THE GREAT WALL
OF BRITAIN

For Rufus

The Great Wall Of Britain

by

Anton Hodge

Dales Large Print Books
Long Preston, North Yorkshire,
BD23 4ND, England.

British Library Cataloguing in Publication Data.

Hodge, Anton
  The great wall of Britain.

  A catalogue record of this book is
  available from the British Library

  ISBN 978-1-84262-600-9 pbk

First published in Great Britain in 2004
by Hayloft Publishing Ltd.

Copyright © 2004 Anton Hodge

Cover illustration © Hayloft Publishing Ltd.

The moral right of the author has been asserted

Published in Large Print 2008 by arrangement with
Hayloft Publishing Ltd.

Dales Large Print is an imprint of Library Magna Books Ltd.

Printed and bound in Great Britain by
T.J. (International) Ltd., Cornwall, PL28 8RW

ACKNOWLEDGEMENTS

In putting this book together, I would like to thank those who read and made comments on the early drafts – especially Jo, Rich and Steve. I would also like to acknowledge the support and efficiency of Dawn at Hayloft.

In addition, special mention should go to Rotters, whose facts about the area never cease to amaze me; to Tony and Keith for a relaxing evening at Monkhill at the end of Day 8; similarly, Andy at Walton, Day 7; to Irene and John, for the meal at Twice Brewed; to all those I met on the way; to Mum and Dad for their support over the years; and finally to Jo and Rufus for putting up with endless visits to the Wall since we moved here.

HADRIAN'S WALL ROUTE

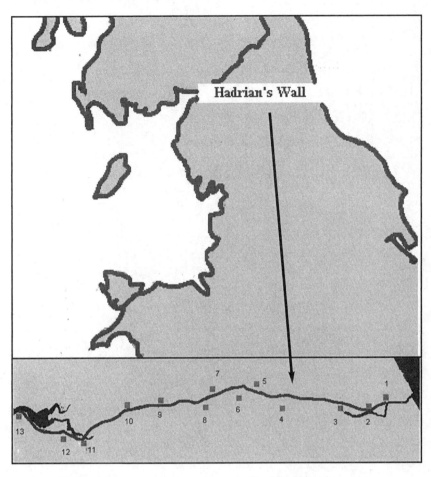

1	Wallsend	8	Vindolanda
2	Newcastle	9	Birdoswald
3	Newburn	10	Walton
4	Corbridge	11	Carlisle
5	Chesters	12	Monkhill
6	Newbrough	13	Bowness-on-Solway
7	Housesteads		

CONTENTS

PROLOGUE

It must have been a dare. Either that or a very cruel joke being played on two unwitting and very fat middle-aged ladies.

I was on the Newcastle Metro – a cleaner, more sanitised version of the Underground – and had hauled my overweight rucksack into an empty carriage going out to Wallsend when I was joined by the two women and their dog. They were mother and daughter, one being around 60, the other about 46 and the dog looked just as old (that's in human, not dog, years). The women shared similar characteristics: hair – short back and sides and an inexplicable tight perm on top – facial features ruined by nicotine, identical dress code (they were wearing England football tops) and weight problem, and of course no sense of personal space, as they decided to ignore the rest of the empty train and squeeze into the small block of four seats where I had just put myself and rucksack.

Already I was beginning to feel the pain in my shoulders having carried the thing a combined total of at least 200 metres, if you included the trip from car to train at Carlisle. Still, only 90-odd miles to go.

I had to tried to be ruthless in my choice of what to take with me and what to leave behind, only being extravagant with the underwear and socks – a pair for each day plus two spares (for emergencies/accidents). Other than that, as well as the trousers I was wearing, I only had one other pair, plus some shorts. T-shirts would have to last two days, although I had also brought an 'evening' one. Other items I had deemed essential were: toothbrush and toothpaste, shampoo (for washing hair and body), deodorant, razor, First Aid kit with extra plasters, camera, notebook and pens, three Ordnance Survey maps, two books, small towel, light jacket, waterproof coat, water bottle and finally some emergency rations such as peanuts, chocolate bars and mini salami sausages. My only hard footwear was on my feet; a pair of reliable walking shoes I had had for a couple of years and which I felt would never let me down. Hanging on my rucksack was a retractable walking stick, which the elderly dog in front of me was now trying to eat.

I smiled at the human owners in a sort of, 'Dogs, huh? What can you do with them?'

way, but was rewarded simply with a scowl from the daughter, who tugged harshly at the lead and swore at the dog. It, meanwhile, had now decided to have sex with my rucksack and its reward was a smack on the nose courtesy of mother's mobile phone.

Eventually my companions left their seats and moved towards the door as the train approached the next station. I remained where I was, as I still had a few stops to go, and watched the indentations in the vacated seats slowly correct themselves. As they got off the train and walked side by side along the platform, I noted that both were wearing number 8 shirts. The train quickly overtook this walking bingo advert and that's when I decided this was more likely a cruel joke played on them by another member of their large and conical-haired family. Perhaps by someone who liked the dog.

So here I was, arriving at Wallsend about to start my adventure of walking the entire length of Hadrian's Wall over a period of eight days in the late summer of 2003. The Wall formed part of the Roman Imperial frontier system in the province of Britannia and is around 75 miles long from Wallsend, four miles east of Newcastle, to Bowness-on-

Solway, some fifteen miles west of Carlisle.

'Why?'

That was a question I was asked rather often in the weeks preceding my journey, and a question I think has many small answers. I should say from the outset that I am no great walker or outdoors type. This conclusion you have probably reached already, having worked out the reasonably leisurely timetable involved in walking 75 miles in eight days. Actually the full walk turned out to be just over 90 miles, but still nothing desperately onerous. When I returned home at the end I found out that a group of runners had passed me somewhere and achieved the distance within two days. However, I was not doing this walk as a race or to prove anything, despite the ribbing I received about a 'mid-life crisis' from colleagues at work.

Living near Carlisle since 1996, I had taken the opportunity of visiting bits of the Wall since then and knew roughly about its purpose and the various bits and pieces to it (oh yes, it was a lot more than just a stone wall, as we will find out) and about some of its history and the myths and tales surrounding it over the past 2,000 years or so. These were some of the things I was hoping to delve deeper into during my week of walking. I hoped also to be able to stop and look at the forts and other remains that are on or near to the Wall.

But as well as looking at the historical stuff and the changing landscape, I also wanted to observe these places as they are now and the people who lived near them. As I travelled across the country on the train from Carlisle to Newcastle I had a sudden fear that perhaps I would not see anything interesting – other than a few old bricks obviously and perhaps a few carvings of Roman genitalia. As I looked around me in the carriage, willing something to happen, some interesting conversation or argument to take place, perhaps, I thought, modern people were rather dull after all.

Of course, I was trying too hard, and once on the Metro and my encounter with the Two Fat Ladies and randy Rex, I realised that this was going to be fun.

Perhaps there is one final reason why I embarked on my Pilgrimage and this dates back to 1984, and the first time I visited the Wall.

I was a schoolboy of fifteen at Perth High School and I absolutely loved some subjects and detested others. Those I detested included PE, anything to do with making things out of wood, metal or cloth, mathematics and anything to do with numbers. In fact numbers actually scared me and I would often have nightmares after a particularly rough Double Maths along the lines of having to do something 456,893,209 times all within the space of 543,781 seconds. As a boy, I used to imagine that everyone had an animal equivalent. Mostly these were genial animals like kittens or horses or magnificent and proud like Siberian tigers or silver-backed gorillas. My Maths teachers however were simply an endless run of docile walruses. The really bad ones were stuffed walruses with cracking skin.

I digress. One of the subjects I loved was Latin, which I took at O-grade (as it then was), Higher and SYS (Sixth Year Studies), before finally getting my MA in 1991. I loved my Latin teacher, Mrs Grant, who also taught me the basics of ancient Greek in my sixth year, and in 1984, she took all of the Latin classes down to Hadrian's Wall for the weekend. At that time I was halfway through my two O-grade years and our class (of nine or ten) were joined by those studying for Highers and SYS, as well as by the newly recruited second year Latin starters, a class which contained some of the most beautiful young ladies in the whole of Perthshire. Needless to say, I spent most of the weekend trying to chat them up and taking little interest in what was soon to become a UNESCO World Heritage Sight. In those days I actually kept a diary and I recently found the entries for the relevant period. They are utterly shameful.

Although the diary does mention that we walked twelve miles (I must have been exaggerating) along the Wall on the Saturday and also went to Vindolanda, Chesters and the Roman Army Museum, there is much more about Pauline, Stephanie and Nicola which I need not go into here. Incidentally I was unsuccessful in my romantic attempts that weekend, although with hindsight, singing the B-sides of Adam Ant records does not seem the most obvious way of wooing women.

My lack of interest in the cultural/ historical side of the trip is proved beyond doubt by the diary entry of 22 October, some weeks afterwards:

'Last Friday we got our corrected work-sheets for Hadrian's Wall back. I got D-, which is not surprising. For example, in answer to the question, "Describe the daily life of a Roman legionary soldier," I put: "It was quite boring as there was not a lot of fighting.'"

So perhaps this trip was partly about making amends, a sort of late apology to Mrs Grant, the woman who inspired me to go on and study the subject at university. Like many following this route I did not make a career out of the Classics, although interest in the subject has stayed with me. My career in fact took a surprising turn after university when I ended up as a local government accountant, thus confronting my demons and fear of numbers (for which read, 'turned up pissed to the wrong day of the Careers Fair').

Whatever the reasons, as I got off the train, after months of preparation, I was now ready for the challenge, the sore feet and the sightseeing, the history and the people. There was only one final decision to be made – should I go straight to my pre-booked bed and breakfast or have a swift pint in the pub first?

1

Wallsend

OK, so all I had done so far was travel the sixty odd miles from home, mainly by train and here I was slacking already. Well, actually yes, but only with purpose. I had deliberately planned to come over the afternoon before and have a walk around Wallsend and a good rest before an early start the next morning, spending the last pre-walk night doing some final reading and getting excited about the prospect of the week or so which lay ahead.

As I left the train I noticed that the place was bilingual: signs were in Latin and English, which did not seem as unconvincing as you might think (is Wales unconvincing?). I struggled down the steps (I was going to have to reassess the weight and contents of my rucksack) and up Station Road towards the guest house where I had booked a room for the night.

I had found this place by searching on the

internet and as it advertised itself as being on the Wall, I felt duty-bound to stay there. In fact it was a couple of hundred metres or so north of the Wall, concealed within a row of terraced houses. Actually it was a terraced house, converted and huge inside, compared with how it looked while standing on the street. It was a lovely place, well decorated and homely (if a little camp), clean and friendly, with lots of literature about the Wall which I would no doubt tuck into later.

The only bizarre thing about the place was that although it seemed to be run by two men, only one of them ever appeared. This was Brian and there was nothing wrong with him, I should say, although he was one of that rare breed (like Cameron of Big Brother 2003 fame) whose accent placed him either as Welsh or Scottish but without much certainty. When I arrived, Brian phoned upstairs and spoke to 'Bart' (I think that was his name) to ask which room I was in, and later on as I passed the private 'out-of-bounds' sector of the house, I would hear Brian address his companion with a series of questions which he himself would answer: 'How is the website going? Oh, hitting a few problems? Never mind, you're a real star,' and so on. Next morning it was Brian who served breakfast (although he gave the impression that the invisible man was the chef) and Brian who stamped my Hadrian's Wall passport and saw me out. As I stood at the door, looking at the stairway, I was tempted to run past him and into the private rooms to see if this guy really existed, but I chickened out.

But it was, as I say, a lovely little B and B. Once I had checked into my room I immediately began to re-pack my lop-sided rucksack and chuck out anything I deemed unnecessary. I manage to lose the razor, though decided I would have one last shave in the morning before setting off. After leafing quickly through some of the brochures/ books about Hadrian's Wall which had been left in the room, I went out into the streets of Wallsend and walked towards Segedunum, the first Roman fort on the Wall.

The Wall was begun on the orders of the Emperor Hadrian some time after he visited Britain in 122 AD. At that time Britain had been part of the Roman Empire for around 80 years, since the invasions of the Emperor Claudius. Julius Caesar had invaded the island some 100 years before that, but had made no real attempt to stay. By the time of Hadrian, most of what we now call England and Wales was under direct Roman rule and a few incursions had been made into Scotland, but Hadrian decided to delineate his Empire and in Britain this was done by building the Wall.

Growing up in Scotland, the propaganda I was fed had always been that the Romans were afraid of the northern tribes and had built the Wall simply as a defensive measure. One thing Mrs Grant had taught me was that this was not true and that there were more complex reasons for its establishment. The only ancient source we have is from a biography perhaps written around the end of the fourth century which states that Hadrian:

'murumque per octoginta milla passuum primus duxit, qui barbaros Romanosque divideret (*Scriptores Historiae Augustae: Vita Hadriani, 11.2*).'

This is usually translated somewhere along the lines of Hadrian being 'the first to build a wall, eighty miles long, to separate the Romans from the barbarians.' And that's about it as regards the ancient sources (and itself some 200 years after the event). Incidentally, descendants of those 'barbarians' need not feel too upset by the apparent term of abuse. The word was borrowed by the Romans from the Greeks, who called anyone who was not Greek a 'barbarian'. As they couldn't speak Greek, their language went something like 'bar-bar-bar-bar-bar...' and so on. Simple!

In modern times there has been much discussion about the purpose of the Wall, and without going into too much detail here, the general consensus is that it was partly a defensive mechanism and partly a border frontier which controlled the flow of people and goods in and out of the province. Although the structure clearly marked Roman territory, there were a number of roads which passed through the Wall and led to Roman forts in 'Caledonia' as the area now known as Scotland was called.

Hadrian's original plan (if indeed he was involved in the detail) was to build the Wall from Newcastle in the east (or Pons Aelius, as it was known, in reverence to Hadrian's family name) to Bowness (Maia) in the west. The Wall in the east was to be built in stone some ten feet wide and fifteen to twenty feet high, depending on whether there was a parapet or not (and we don't know if there was). The stone wall would stretch from Newcastle to the River Irthing, just on the Cumbria-Northumberland border, where, due to difficulties in obtaining limestone for the mortar and other materials, the remainder of the Wall would be a thicker turf one. The Romans built from west to east and by the time they had reached the area now known as Planetrees (just east of Chollerford), they decided that the ten foot thickness was not really required and it then became around eight feet thick. Later on the Turf Wall in Cumbria was also replaced by a Stone Wall. In front was a ditch around ten feet deep and thirty wide.

So Wallsend was not on the original plan and was only added some time afterwards with the narrower Wall being built east from Newcastle.

The fort itself was known as Segedunum, which is apparently Celtic for 'Strong Fort' or perhaps 'Victory Fort' and the word is now incorporated into the town's official letter-heading. Until very recently there was not much to see. Once the Romans had left these shores, as with many places on the Wall, the valuable stone was largely whisked away to help with grand buildings, in this case the Saxon priories at Jarrow and Tynemouth. Later the area became farmland (as it had been before the Wall was built) before coal was mined from the eighteenth century. Everyone, including the Romans, has always known there was coal there, but it was buried too deep for any mining before this time. Thus by the beginning of the nineteenth century, the area on which Segedunum stood had become a bustling pit village. At the end of the nineteenth century, the area was covered by housing which lasted until the 1970s, when it was pulled down and excavations of the fort began. Since then, interest in the Roman heritage has been much aroused, perhaps in making up for lost time. These days you can visit what has been excavated of the fort and see a replica of the Wall at its full size. There is also a visitor centre and an observation tower where you can look at the outline of the entire fort which has been painstakingly marked out down below.

Walking around, I was also struck by the street names and other references to the Romans. As well as the obvious name of the town itself and the bilingual signs at the Metro Station (strange to see the Latin for 'No Smoking', when clearly the Romans did not have the benefit of Sir Walter Raleigh's overseas booty, though I searched in vain for a sign advertising chips or baked potatoes), there were numerous streets named 'Hadrian' or 'Praetorian' or 'Tiberius' (a pervy emperor who died nearly 100 years before the Wall – how did he get there?). There was the Forum indoor shopping centre and even a carpet shop using the name 'Walter Wall's Carpets'.

The most striking aspect about Wallsend, however, is of course the massive Swan Hunter shipyards, which straddle the course of the Wall, just where it ran down to the Tyne. Shipbuilding has been part of Wallsend since 1759. In 1894 the world's first turbine-engined ship, the *Turbinia*, was built here and in 1906 the massive liner, the *Mauretania*, was launched at Wallsend. I have to admit that before I visited, these facts meant nothing to me. However there is something quite magnificent about the view from the end of the fort, the perfect juxtaposition, as you look out towards the giant cranes on the river bank. Of course the massive cranes also seem to belong to a bygone era (technology these days is hidden and largely unseen), although there is still a large shipbuilding programme on the Tyne. Wallsend is really a place where its days of glory are in the past, but I rather liked the nostalgia and the way the past is now being used as a new business opportunity, as well as helping us find out all about those Romans.

Musing on such things, I finally went for

that drink and popped into what seemed to be the only pub in town. Everything in Wallsend is 'big': the cranes, the ships they built, the Roman Fort and the full-size replica Wall. The Barras pub on Station Road was no exception. It did however appear to be letting the town down by refusing to take part in the Roman Name Game, being stubbornly known as 'The Ianson'.

I ordered a Becks and was asked if I wanted a pint. I nodded, expecting the German beer to be on tap, but was handed a pint of very English bitter. OK, I thought, this is the hard north-east. You are probably not allowed to drink soft foreign bottled beers here, but a minute later I saw someone else with such a bottle. I found a quiet table in the corner, opposite an elderly gentleman who was unable to stop hiccuping, even though he tried every supposed method, including drinking his beer upside down, holding his breath and, in a strange variation of one of the other cures, trying to give himself a shock. At least I presume that was what he was doing when he a) repeatedly dropped his keys down his back and/or b) occasionally turned his head sharply to one side, shouting 'Yaargh!!!' Having drained my glass I approached the bar again, determined to get my Becks this time.

'Can I have a Becks please?'

Nod. She went off. Thirty seconds later I was handed my second pint of bitter.

I shrugged my shoulders, took the pint and returned to my seat, noticing that most of the others in the pub were drinking Becks, even the skin-heads in the corner.

Unwilling to be too despondent I took out my book and began to read again about the Wall.

As I said earlier, the Wall is only one part of the Roman Imperial frontier system in the area of what is now northern England and central Scotland. The Romans had arrived there shortly after their invasion in 43 AD and by the beginning of the second century had penetrated as far north as the Scottish Highlands. There were three legions in Britain, the II, VI and XX, each with around 5,000 men based at Caerleon (South Wales), Chester and York. A road ran from York to Corbridge and beyond, later known as Dere Street, and a further main Roman road ran east to west from Corbridge to Carlisle. At both ends of the east-west road, now called the Stanegate, or 'stone road,' there were Roman forts and settlements, with a few on the way too.

When Hadrian decided to build his Wall, sometime around 122 AD, it was positioned just north of the Stanegate. Soldiers from the three legions built the Wall, taking somewhere between eight and ten years, before returning to their bases further south. The soldiers who manned the frontier were from much smaller units of infantry and cavalry, although they still probably numbered over 15,000 men.

At first the forts on the Stanegate (such as at Carlisle, Chesterholm [Vindolanda] and Corbridge) provided military assistance to the Wall. On the Wall itself, in front of which lay a defensive ditch, there was a series of 'milecastles' where the soldiers could shelter and between these, two smaller 'turrets'. Thus there was some form of shelter for most of the length every third of a mile.

At some point after the Wall had been begun, we have seen how a number of revisions were incorporated into the plans. One of these was to extend the Wall from its original eastern base towards Wallsend. Another was to build a series of forts actually on the Wall itself. There are fifteen or sixteen of these, depending on how you count them and these combined with the Stanegate forts, plus others further east at South Shields, further west at Old Carlisle, Maryport and Papcastle, and to the north at Netherby, Birrens, Bewcastle, Risingham and High Rochester, to provide a strong and impressive defensive (or aggressive) military force. As the Wall forts were an afterthought, we know that in places the milecastles and turrets already built were partially or fully destroyed to accommodate them.

Another amendment to the plan was to build, or rather dig, a large ditch just to the south of the Wall, known confusingly since the times of the Venerable Bede (672-735 AD) as the 'vallum', which is Latin for 'wall'. This vallum was nearly ten feet deep and twenty feet wide, with a flat bottom of around eight feet. The excavated soil was piled up in two mounds either side of the ditch, some thirty feet away from it. Thus the width of the entire structure was some 120 feet. Sometimes this vallum was placed only a few metres away from the Wall, but in other places, depending on the terrain, it is nearly half a mile from it.

If there has been disagreement concerning the purpose of the Wall, then agreement regarding that of the vallum is even less easy to find, although again there seems to be a general consensus, this time that the vallum was intended to mark the boundary between the military and civilian zones, south of the wall. At the forts there were causeway crossings and large gateways, but at the milecastles, the northern mound only had been cut through, leading to the Roman Military Way, a twenty foot wide road which ran between the Wall and Vallum, traces of which can still be seen. Incidentally, the vallum does not go any further east than Newcastle, so it may have been built before the extension to Wallsend.

Thus the whole system known as Hadrian's Wall consisted of the following, from north to south:

a ditch

the Wall, with forts, milecastles and turrets

the Roman Military Way

the 'vallum' with its earth-mounds either side

forts

Further south lay the Stanegate, running from Corbridge to Carlisle, with additional Roman settlements which acted as supply bases for the soldiers on the fort.

As I finished my second unasked-for pint, I reflected how, on my walk, I was hoping to see evidence of all of these.

I hesitated before going to the bar again, but not too long, and I aimed to stand in front of the barmaid who had not yet served me. Just as I got there, one of the skinheads jumped in front of me to order a gin and tonic, and so I was forced once again to try with my adversary.

'Yes, love, another pint?'

The skinhead looked at me. The music stopped. The man with the hiccups shouted, 'Yaargh!'

Before I could answer she said, 'Sorry, love, it's just gone off. If you can wait a minute, he's just gonna change the barrel.'

Huh?

'The Becks is off...? It's in a barrel...? It's...?' I mumbled, confused.

'Becks?' she asked, genuinely surprised.

'Yes, Becks. Have you got any Becks?'

Something happened inside her head and she started to apologise. Apparently she thought I had been ordering 'Ex' or 'Exhibition', a local beer. I told her not to worry, but as I walked away from the bar, finally with my Becks, the skinhead whispered to me, 'She always does that.'

After having some food at the pub, I found myself strangely in the mood for another walk – surprising really as I had some ten miles to walk the next day – and ventured outside. However, it had started raining – not a good omen, so I went in search of a shop where I could buy some water and further emergency provisions. I found a little shop down a side-street where two men were laughing hysterically about the size of the print in some local trade magazine.

'Can you read that?' asked one of them as he thrust the magazine in front of my eyes. I couldn't, but simply because the page was less than three inches from my eyes. I wasn't sure if I should respond, but didn't need to when the other shouted out through tears and giggles, 'No job too small? No fucking print too small, more like.' The guy who served me did not stop laughing until well after I had left the shop.

The rain had killed any desire for an evening walk, so I returned to the bed and breakfast, to catch up on my reading and pore over the Ordnance Survey maps. However, by 10.30, I found myself back in the Ianson, only a hundred metres away, for last orders. This time there was no difficulty in getting my Becks, although the barmaid (who was still on duty) was telling everyone about her/my earlier mistake. The skinheads were still in, drinking what looked like fruit cocktails. With parasols.

I sat down at the only available table and listened to the drunken argument going on beside me between a husband and wife. The problem centred somehow on the fact that the husband had bought two pints of Exhibition and the wife had a problem with this. I began to suspect that she had been after a bottle of Becks, but it turned out that she had only wanted a half and he was made to go up to the bar and ask for an empty half-pint glass, into which she poured half of her pint. There then followed five minutes of shouting at each other in monosyllabic and occasionally foul language, before he, bizarrely, urged her to be quiet with a gesture of directing his outstretched palms towards her, put on his hat, stated very slowly in a quiet voice, 'The problem seems to be that you are always upsetting the equilibrium,' and took his hat off once more.

She exploded and in her alcohol-infused Wallsend accent, I was unable to make out much of her response, other than that it contained the word 'equilibrium' two or three times.

One thing I had noticed earlier in the pub was the relatively high proportion of disabled and wheelchair-using punters and the Ianson certainly had spent a great deal of effort (and money) ensuring that there were adequate facilities for the disabled, such as ramps, separate toilets and so on. The people sitting on the other side of the arguing spouses had wisely moved away and they were replaced by three women, one of whom was in a wheelchair. Suddenly the arguments stopped and the two broke off their hostilities to become the most civil and polite, happily married couple in town, making conversation and joking with the new arrivals, particularly the lady with the disability. I did not know whether to find this charming or patronising (and the young lady and her companions gave no clue either), but actually found it quite warming in a strange sort of way. My thoughts were disturbed by the very loud live music which was now being produced by a man, woman and karaoke machine on stage, and I took this as a cue to leave and head for bed, although to be fair, the singers were quite impressive.

Next morning I woke up and after a very fair full English breakfast (the 'Northumberland' – whatever that was – was off), set out once more to the fort at Segedunum and thence towards Newcastle.

2

Wallsend to Newcastle

'Let me at the outset disclaim all pretence that there is anything noteworthy in walking the length of the Roman Wall.' So said David Harrison in 1956, before going on to contradict himself and write an entire book *Along Hadrian's Wall* which I had found in Carlisle Library. This is justly described on the jacket cover as 'a highly readable book', and is worth seeking out, particularly for his asides and social commentary on both the Romans and his own times as well as astute and sometime unfair remarks regarding the places he visited. On the place I had just left he remarks: 'I did not think much of Wallsend, though I must not be too hard on a borough which is no doubt doing its best.' On the now-reformed pub opening hours, and after being rejected at The Errington Arms (Portgate), he says: 'What earthly good do our legislators think they achieve by preventing travellers obtaining an innocent drink at any time? Do they really think that Englishmen would only make beasts of themselves without such restrictions?' I wonder what he would have made of TV programmes such as *Club Reps*, which I had watched in the bed and breakfast the night before as I waited to fall asleep?

One of my favourite comments in his book, however, is where he remarks on the high sophistication of Roman washing and sanitary habits, some of which disappeared when the Romans left and took until the late 1800s to resume: 'It is distressing to reflect that after Roman days most people, medieval monks, proud nobles, even Shakespeare and Dr Johnson, might have offended our modern noses.'

Harrison was not the first to walk along and write about the Wall and a few of the more notable authors are mentioned below. In 1599, William Camden surveyed the whole country and published his *Britannia* (in Latin, and translated into English first in 1610). Camden's book is interestingly split into sections based on the ancient tribes of Britain, thus the chapter entitled 'Vallum, The Pict's Wall', can be found next to the section on the Brigantes, a tribe based in what is now northern England. He was unable or unwilling to visit personally the central section of the Wall, due to what he described as 'rank robbers', more commonly known as the Border Reivers (see later, Chapter 6).

In 1801, a 78 year old from Birmingham, William Hutton, wrote his book *The History of the Roman Wall, Which Crosses the Island of Britain, From The German Ocean to The Irish Sea, Describing Its Ancient State, and Its Appearance in the Year 1801.* This is a lovely little book which has recently been reprinted, confusingly as *The First Man To Walk Hadrian's Wall 1802* by Frank Graham of Newcastle (1990). In it, Hutton not only describes his walk along the Wall (both ways) but also his journey from Birmingham and back again, on foot, a round trip of 601 miles!

Hutton was accompanied by his daughter Catherine (who was then 45) from Birmingham as far as the Lake District, where she was doing her own walk. Catherine did not however walk from Birmingham to the Lakes. Whereas her father would rise at 4am each morning and set off on foot, Catherine would set out at 7am, riding on horseback (pillion, behind a servant) and catch William up where they would breakfast at an inn. After he had rested for two hours, William would then set off again, meeting up with his daughter at the end of the day at the place where they would spend the night. Catherine noted in a preface to a later edition of the book that: 'he would not allow me to walk by his side, either on foot or on horseback; not even through a town. The only time I ever did walk with him was through the street of Warrington; and then, of my own accord, I kept a little behind, that I might not influence his step.' This odd behaviour lasted until they reached Penrith, where they split up and went their separate ways.

The whole journey lasted just over a month, from 4 July until 7 August, causing Hutton to remark: 'Perhaps I am the first man that ever travelled the whole length of this Wall, and probably the last that will ever attempt it.'

Both Camden and Hutton lived in the time when it was believed that Hadrian had only built the 'vallum' and that the Wall itself was actually a later addition, usually attributed to the Emperor Septimius Severus (who ruled 193-211 AD). It was not until the Rev John Hodgson (*The History of Northumberland*, 1832) that this theory was dispelled, and later publicised in John Collingwood Bruce's publications after 1850.

Collingwood Bruce is attributed as the great grandmaster of the Wall and his *Handbook of the Roman Wall* was first published in 1863. It has been revised and updated over the years, to take account of new discoveries, most notably by Prof Sir Ian Richmond and latterly by Charles M Daniels in 1978. This 1978 version was one of the two books I had decided to take with me on my walk, and is an invaluable guide to the Wall and the other parts of the frontier system in the north of England and south Scotland.

In 1922 Jessie Mothersole's *Hadrian's Wall* was published – a written account of a walk along the wall, complete with sketches and drawings by this remarkable woman. Ms Mothersole's journey began on the hottest day of the year after travelling on the overnight sleeper from London. Arriving at 5am, she set off towards Wallsend, before retracing her footsteps westwards. By midday the weather was so hot, the gutters ran with molten tar – or so she says. On the first day she intended to stay at the Temperance Hotel at Harlow Hill and had sent a postcard there well in time. However the postcard arrived back at her home, some 400 miles away, marked 'return to sender', roughly about the same time she was discovering that the hotel had been closed down during the Great War. So on she went, aiming for the Robin Hood Inn at East Wallhouses. This was closed, although she did manage to find lodgings at a house nearby. It would take me a day and a half to cover the same ground.

Jessie lived in a very different age. All along the route she had difficulty getting any hospitality at inns or hotels and generally ended up staying at farm houses where the people were usually friendly.

Unlike Hutton, she did manage to get a drink (of milk) at the Errington Arms – paid for by the local postman. She had less luck at the Twice Brewed Inn (no food for her: anything she could see was for the owners), the Traveller's Rest at Banks (closed), the Lanercost Temperance Hotel (full), and the Stag at Crosby (no beds, no food, but she was allowed in to sit down and write a letter). At the Near Boot Inn (Tarraby, Carlisle), she was 'attacked' by a pack of greyhounds who stole her lunch. The owners were unwilling to sell her any food or drink until they heard this story (turns out the dogs probably belonged to the pub).

Jessie Mothersole also gives an interesting viewpoint on the significance of walls: 'In all ages, the building of walls has marked a stage of advance in the evolution of the human character, in so far as it has meant a progress from the offensive to the defensive position.' I'm not sure, after the experiences of Berlin, Northern Ireland, and, more recently in the Middle East, that there would be much agreement nowadays.

As regards more recent books, there is the entertaining Harrison, mentioned above and also *A Walk Along The Wall*, written by Hunter Davies in 1972. If I am being honest it was this book which inspired me to write about walking the Wall. Davies' book is a fascinating 'study of its time', so to speak, and he somehow managed to get himself meetings with a number of the aristocracy who lived in the area. So far it had been interesting to compare what had happened to Wallsend in the intervening thirty years and I was looking forward to other comparisons. Davies had arrived in Wallsend during a shipbuilders' strike. Coincidentally, Jessie Mothersole had passed through there during a coal miners' strike.

I had read two other books as part of my research. The first is *Hadrian's Magic Stones* by Arnold N Patchett, written in 1989, again an interesting 'study of its time', based on driving and walking along the Wall and the surrounding area. Finally, a different sort of book, but also based on a walk along the Wall, is Tony Hopkins' *Walking The Wall*, from 1993. Although only four years after Patchett's book, its style and language seem much more modern. This is also a book for nature lovers and is full of sketches and drawings made on the journey.

All of these writers had made the trip from east to west (even Patchett who went House-steads to Bowness, then Wallsend to House-steads) as I was about to do, and which is the way as described in the official National Trail publication, which was the other book I had brought with me.

The Hadrian's Wall Path National Trail has been long in the planning, but it finally opened on 23 May 2003, and for most of its way, it shadows the line of the Wall. There are places where it does not follow the Wall, probably for good reason – as I was soon to find out. Incidentally, although I had been aware of talk of this trail, I did not realise it would open in May 2003 until after I had decided to do my walk in the following August: a useful coincidence, and one which meant I would probably have an easier time of it than previous walkers who sometimes had 'difficulty finding places to stay/eat/

drink or easily found hostility among the local population. At least in 2003, they would be ready for me.

There was only one reason why I was walking from east to west. It wasn't because, as I live in the Carlisle area, I preferred the idea of 'walking home' more than the alternative. Some of the other writers who went this way have explained their reasons such as:

– the better public transport access to Wallsend compared with Bowness;

– there is more to see at the western end and the scenery there is more beautiful than the grime of Newcastle;

– because others had done it this way and that was the way most of the guidebooks (such as that of Collingwood Bruce) had been written;

– the Romans probably built this way, apart, obviously, from the later extension between Newcastle and Wallsend;

– the numbering system for the forts and turrets goes from east to west.

However, my simple reason was nothing to do with these. It was to do with the sun and my lack of desire to walk into it (I would mainly be walking in the morning and early-mid afternoon). As you might expect, as I walked through the rain a few hours after arriving in Wallsend, I wondered whether the sun would indeed be of any nuisance at all.

Walking now past Segedunum and the Swan Hunter Shipyards on the Friday morning as others were going to work, the sun was shining brightly. Across the road from the fort is a possible replica piece of Wall, to its full height. I say 'possible replica' as this bit has a walkway and parapet – something we do not know for sure. There are also various 'finishes' to parts of the replica, again because we are not sure. There is certainly evidence that the Wall was plastered or whitewashed – which, if true, would have made an impressive and frightening sight for the local tribes, particularly in the moonlight.

The official trail takes you down to the banks of the Tyne and away from the Wall, before rejoining it some eleven miles later. The National Trail Guidebook promises: 'a route packed with interest and an ideal introduction to the city that grew up beside the river. There are not only urban pleasures to enjoy, for there is no shortage of wildlife along the way.' I presume by this they meant butterflies and an occasional seagull which had strayed inland, which really wasn't worth deviating from the Wall for. Were I to have followed the path I would have missed the site of the second and third forts, a Celtic temple, the first bit of vallum and a vallum crossing, the first bits of Wall, a museum and a wonderful shop on the outskirts of Newcastle known perfectly adequately as 'Egg and Potato Shop'. A promised sighting of herds of Tasmanian Wolves or Russian sabre-toothed bears might have tempted me to miss all of this, but not really some flying caterpillars, no matter how colourful their wings. Oh, and my way was slightly shorter. Possibly by around two miles.

So I set off through Wallsend down the A187, which I was pleased to note was a relatively quiet road. This road soon changed its name to Fossway, confirming to me that I was on the right track, as this derives from the Latin word for ditch. Other place-names inspired by the Wall included Brough Park in Walker, where greyhound racing takes place, from the Old English word for 'earthen defences' and sometimes 'fort'. This was a word which was to appear in a number of guises later in the walk. I had also passed the rather sinister-looking pub, the Turbinia, named after that ship built in Wallsend which I mentioned earlier.

Walking towards Newcastle, traffic began to become increasingly heavy. Crossing over a hill-top roundabout just before Byker, I went down a very busy road with a frigheningly small pavement and vehicles whizzing past me at what seemed like 100mph. Reluctantly I turned back and found myself in the main street of the area known as Byker. Worried that I had now deviated from the true path of the Wall, I found another quieter road, just south of the Metro station. To my right I saw the famous/infamous Byker Wall, a housing development nearly a mile long, which attempted to marry the solution of high density accommodation with an acceptable environment. Behind the outside walls are gardens and walkways, and coincidentally, the day I finished my walk, a report on BBC News mentioned that the Byker Wall had been suggested for listed building status.

As I walked down the hill past the station, suddenly three skinheads came running towards me. They did not look like the type who drank G and Ts or cocktails with umbrellas – more leaded petrol types – and I actually felt a little bit uncomfortable. I remember noticing that the sun had now disappeared behind a cloud and that there was a bit of a breeze. My rucksack suddenly felt very heavy. They continued running towards me and slowed down to walking pace just two metres in front. One of them opened his mouth and shouted at the top of his voice, 'Giggsy! Giggsy!' I wondered if I would be needing those extra pants and hoped that they didn't nick my underwear. However, the three continued walking and went right past me. I half expected to feel something cold and sharp between my shoulder blades but when I eventually had enough courage to turn around, realised that they were approaching this 'Giggsy' who was a few hundred metres further on. Although they had been so close to me, in fact had almost walked through me, they just hadn't seen me. I was just being paranoid, and with spirits lifted (and the sun re-emerging) I noticed a police station immediately to my right. Nevertheless I decided to make my way back to the main Byker street, which I had to do by going around the police station.

A policeman came out of the front door and stood watching me as I hurried on, but then I felt the sun disappear once again. I looked up and sure enough another short-haired person was approaching me. However I saw with some relief that he was older (mid-50s) and was carrying two plastic shopping bags. But then he looked up and saw me and hesitated. He eyed me up and down and then started looking about him, before finally catching sight of the policeman who was still there watching me. At this the mid-50s guy visibly shrugged his shoulders in a 'you've got nothing on me, guv' kind of fashion and continued on his way. Again, the sun reappeared and I felt it burning into the back of my neck. Relieved, I reached the main street once more.

The earliest inhabitants in the area were here around 8,000 years ago. These were the so-called Mesolithic, or Middle Stone Age, people – the 'hunter-gatherers'. Four thousand years later, early man began farming, using stone tools to clear the large areas of forest which covered Britain.

The Bronze Age, from 2,000 BC, and then the Iron Age, refer simply to the advances in tool making, but such advances were not enough to prevent the invasions of the Celts some time after 900 BC. This was not a single event, rather a series of incursions lasting for centuries.

By the time the Romans arrived, what we now know as the north of England was dominated by the Brigantes. This Celtic tribe occupied both sides of the Tyne and it is highly likely that the area now swallowed by Newcastle, with its favourable lowland site – ideal for river crossings – was also occupied by the Brigantes.

When the Romans came, sometime after 70 AD, they did not make immediate use of Newcastle's bridging opportunities, building a crossing further west at Corbridge instead. Eventually, with the building of the Wall, a bridge was constructed here too, and of course the fort, both named Pons Aelius. This is the first solid evidence we have of the beginning of Newcastle.

Little is known of what happened to the settlement once Roman power declined, until the Norman invasions after 1066. However we do know that in 1072, following excursions into Scotland, William the Conqueror passed through here on his way back down south. He was delayed, unable to ford the Tyne because of floods, suggesting that the Roman Bridge – indeed any bridge – no longer existed.

In 1080, Robert Curthose, the eldest son of William, was sent here and he built a 'new castle', and a new bridge, and after that the town seems to have developed, taking its name from the first of these renovations. Newcastle became a busy port, exporting wool (which was medieval England's biggest industry) and, from the thirteenth century, coal. The shipbuilding industry began as early as 1294.

William the Conqueror had encountered difficulties crossing the Tyne, but Newcastle is now a city of bridges, and not only those which go across the river. I passed over a couple, over a very busy confusion of roads joining one another and reached the quieter centre of the city. Making my way up the pedestrianised area towards the university, I had now entered market research territory. There seemed to be more women with clip-boards (yes, very few men doing this) than actual shoppers. I kept my head down and pushed on, but was unable to avoid contact for very long. Fortunately there seemed to be some sort of weeding-out system, although it took me some time to work this out.

'Excuse me sir, are you a coffee drinker?'

'Yes?'

'Well, if you would like to come into this building here, we have free coffee to give away and perhaps you could answer a few questions about your favourite brands?'

'Well, actually,' I said, pointing to my rucksack, 'I'm a bit busy at the moment.'

'It'll only take a minute, sir, and you can have a wee rest from your walking?'

It was tempting, but I've been involved in this sort of thing before. One minute you are in there, resting your feet and shoulders and drinking Golden Colombian from a plastic cup; the next you are signing up for a timeshare in Spain or have bought a Japanese bubble car at a 'favourable rate of interest' for the first two years.

'Sorry,' I said before muttering something about keeping to a schedule, quite unnecessarily mentioning raising money for sick children, then put my head down and moved on.

Ten seconds later, 'Excuse me, sir, have you bought a new car in the last two years?'

I hedged my bets, 'No?'

'OK, thank you sir, sorry to trouble you.'

Aha, so that was the system.

For the remaining length of the street I was bombarded with several questions about my hobbies, tastes, personal hygiene and political bent. Was I a vegetarian? Did I vote at the last election? Did I use roll-on or spray-on deodorant? My reply, 'Neither', was met with a scowl of distaste. And so on until I crossed the road to enter the grounds of the museum.

The Museum of Antiquities was worth the short diversion and the consumer interrogation. Here, where entry is free, there is an interesting collection of artifacts from the Wall and it was a useful introduction and context-placer for the next seven days. Mainly it is a collection of carved and inscribed stones, but the two most impressive sights were a scale model of the entire wall, where I spent twenty minutes gazing at the detail and looking with wonder at what I was about to embark on; and a replica of the Temple of Mithras which is at Brocolitia, and which I would see on the following Monday.

Back near the centre of the city, I passed through 'Chinatown' and along the remains of the medieval city wall, passed where the second fort on the Wall, Pons Aelius, had been (there is absolutely nothing to see nowadays), before beginning my long ascent of Benwell Hill, via the Westgate Road. This was tougher than I was prepared for and I was forced to rest a few times, sitting on thoughtfully-placed benches and looking towards where the vallum had been, just south of the road. Before this point, it is assumed that the marshy nature of the ground (the 'ker' in names such as Walker and Byker derives from a word meaning marsh) either made it impossible or unnecessary to build the vallum. It is also believed that none of the turrets, two of which were placed elsewhere between each milecastle, were built here.

The Westgate Road became busier, in the sense that there were more shops and houses, through which I could look to my left down to the imposing Tyne Valley. Most of these shops however seemed to be closed or even boarded up, apart from hairdressers, sun-bed and tanning places and of course pubs.

As I neared the top of the hill, I came to the site of the third fort on the Wall, Condercum, appropriately from the Celtic meaning 'good views on all sides' and now known as Benwell. Again there is nothing to see of the fort itself, but just to the south-west, in a street called Broomridge Avenue, there are the remains of a temple to the Celtic God Antenociticus. I had seen some original remains from this temple an hour earlier in the University Museum and the altars on show at Benwell are replicas, but as it was the first piece of Wall-type evidence I had seen since the rather sanitised remains of Segedunum, it was nevertheless impressive.

Another notable sight at Benwell is the vallum crossing in Denhill Park. When the vallum was built, it diverted south around most of the forts on the Wall and this is what happened here. Crossings were installed, i.e. the vallum was filled in, and a road led through an impressive gateway into the fort.

Going back up the Westgate Road again, I reached Denton and came to the first piece of actual Wall, some nineteen metres long. It was here that the entertaining Harrison, on seeing the Wall surrounded by 'glaring' advertising hoardings, once again lost control of his anger management: 'Why, one asks, must so much of what we have to see be spoiled by advertisements? ... why, for instance, should our buses be plastered with feeble jokes and our stations uglified by those grotesque longshanks drinking rum? And why, in particular, are escalators dedicated to women's underwear?'

Clearly old Harrison had a few issues regarding public transport and lingerie, which, to our loss, he doesn't expand on.

Nearby there are the first remains of a turret, known as Denton Hall Turret, or Turret 7b. The numbering system of the turrets and milecastles is very useful, giving the walker some indication of distance and progress. Each milecastle is, surprisingly enough, one Roman mile from the previous one, and was really a miniature fort, with accommodation for up to thirty men. The turrets were much smaller and, unlike the mile-castles, did not have gates through the Wall, and were really just observation posts. Milecastles were numbered from east to west, and the two turrets in between were labelled 'a' and 'b'. Thus from east to west you pass Milecastle 7, then Turret 7a, then Turret 7b, then Milecastle 8, Turret 8a, Turret 8b, Milecastle 9, and so on. Not all of the milecastle and turret remains have been found, but their position can be easily guessed, thanks to the strict sequencing along the Wall. Each Roman mile was slightly shorter than a modern mile, at 1,686 yards or 1,540 metres, but as I say, following this system gives you a pretty good understanding of distance and how far you have walked.

Stepping over the low railing to have a closer look at the Wall here I suddenly lost my balance and my rucksack pulled me back to the ground where I landed with a thud. Fortunately the bulk of my pack had given me a soft landing and, realising, that I was unhurt, I had a sudden attack of the giggles. I decided that it was time for something to eat, so sat down for a while and ate a chocolate bar and a bag of salted peanuts. Feeling much better, I stood up, rather too quickly, fastened my rucksack around me and promptly fell over once again. This time I was a little embarrassed, as I knew I was being watched by a group of three elderly ladies on their way to buy some eggs and/or potatoes at the nearby Egg and Potato Shop, and so I hurried on, under the sprawling A1, past a longer stretch of Wall and along the A69 for a few minutes before veering off at a minor road, the B6528, towards Walbottle. Once in Walbottle, I stopped at the pub on the right hand side of the road ('The Original Masons' – a humorous reference to the Roman builders?) and enjoyed a glass of water and a Budweiser, knowing that I only had two more miles to walk that day.

It was still only lunchtime and food was being served, but I was content with a liquid lunch for the time being. As I walked to the loo, I was aware of two strange feelings. Firstly, having taken my rucksack off, my legs turned to jelly and I actually seemed to have forgotten how to walk. Eyes from every other table followed me out of curiosity, as my knees shot off in opposite directions and I only just managed to avoid landing on the floor again. The second feeling was less odd, but also less welcome. The soles of my feet were beginning to ache and there was a sharp cutting pain at the bottom of each heel; the beginning of blisters, I feared.

After finishing my beer I decided to move on, eager now to get to my hotel in Newburn, a couple of miles away, and unfortunately a mile south of the Wall. As I walked towards Throckley, the alcohol had a lovely anaesthetic effect on the pain emanating from my feet, and I made a list of what I would do when I got there – a bath/shower, soaking of the feet, plasters, cool drink, walk down to the Riverside Country Park, compare notes with a few fellow walkers who had followed the official trail (which passes through Newburn), have a lovely meal, a glass of wine, meet some locals, and a long sleep.

In the end, I was, you could say, a bit disappointed.

At Throckley, I turned down the hill and entered Newburn. As at Wallsend, I was heading for a Station Road, but the railway line was clearly on the other side of the river in Ryton. After searching for half an hour, I asked someone where the Newburn Hotel was. His reply did not fill me with confidence.

'Hotel? Hah! Well, the pub is down there. Hotel?'

After another minute or so, I found it. It was a hotel-pub, a bit run down, lower windows smashed, dogs killing each other outside, you know the sort of place. However I had nowhere else to go and so, ignoring the pub entrance, I rang the bell of the other main door.

I ought to say that the people were friendly enough and very accommodating, especially as they hadn't expected me this early (it was around 3pm). I put my luggage in my room (which hadn't been made up yet) and took my chances in the bar. Everyone was drunk and there was no sense of feeling threatened, particularly, as I said, with the hotel staff being so friendly. If anything they were a little too obsequious. There was no bottled beer so I had a pint of John Smiths, which was pretty horrible.

Eventually I managed to get up to my room where I lay down for a bit, wondering what to do. My feet did have two large blisters on each heel, so I washed them in the hand sink (the room was not en-suite), had a wash (not the long-desired bath), put on some fresh clothes and eventually, with feet plastered and encased in extra socks, ventured outside to have a look at Newburn.

This was the place of a great battle in 1640. Three years previously, Charles I, king of both England and Scotland, imposed the Prayer Book on Scotland, which was seen north of the border as just a bit too what we might still call 'high' in Church terms, or Anglican-Catholic. The Scots decided to try and restore the purity of the Kirk and eventually this led to fighting in the borders, where, at Newburn, Charles' army was defeated by the rebels. The Scots had captured Newcastle, and these events led to both the recall of the English Parliament (which had not met since 1629) and also to great damage to the king's credibility. Civil War broke out two years after the Battle of Newburn, and seven years after that the King was executed.

I walked out of the hotel and towards the river to enter the Tyne Riverside Country Park. This was a pleasant contrast to the grim highlights of the town, with a footpath leading to a children's playground and small visitor centre. Across the water, the river bank is covered by trees with a church spire piercing the horizon. It felt wonderfully peaceful, except for the buzzing of the electricity pylons overhead. Presently I came to a very nice pub, the Keelman, which was serving food and so I sat in the beer garden, reading the guidebooks and cursing the internet search engine which had picked out the Newburn Hotel above this place, as it also did accommodation.

My feet were now very sore and for the next three hours I did not move, other than to keep asking for Becks and the occasional alkohol-frei Bitburger (well, I didn't want to be too hung over the next day). I also watched two 'Weekend Dads' meeting up to have a pint after a day of looking after their children. One of these, a boy of about six, clearly objected to the other, a girl of about five, and every so often his objections turned into physical violence. The girl was terrified, but the Dads didn't seem to notice what was going on. There was a look of sheer terror in her face when her father suggested that she and her 'friend' go off and play in the nearby playground. She refused and received a couple of whacks on the legs for her troubles. One from her father who didn't want his drinking spoiled by the chatter of children, and one from the boy, who now clearly thought it was open season. He in turn was whacked on the legs by his father and the howling started. The sun had gone down, so I moved inside and ordered some food.

As I waited for my tuna mayonnaise salad to arrive, an elderly gentleman was trying to sell numbers in the pub's Lottery Bonus Ball sweep, explaining that this week was a roll over, although his son had won the previous week. There was indeed a roll over in the national game, as someone eventually pointed out to him, but this had no effect on the pub's mini-version where the maximum prize would be £49 and no more. Finally understanding this, the poor old man looked totally crushed, and immediately guilty and started off in search of those to whom he had sold numbers, presumably to apologise and offer a full refund. Right on queue the juke box started up with a solemn dirge sung by Celine Dion.

Apart from the blisters, the bruised soles of my feet, the being woken up in the night (more later), the rain on the more exposed parts of the Wall and various other small tortures, the one thing which was difficult to take during my walk was my constant exposure to very bad music in pubs. Every pub seemed to have a decidedly dodgy 70s compilation tape, which always featured classics such as *Save All Your Kisses For Me*, *Chirpy Chirpy Cheep Cheep* and the likes. There was also occasionally a 'the Worst of the 80s' compilation. Now I am a child of the 1980s and some of the best music ever produced came from that decade, from Adam Ant to ZZ Top (well the videos anyway). This was the decade of Duran Duran, The Smiths, Jesus and Mary Chain and many other great bands. The stuff I heard ignored all of these, concentrating on Nick Kamen, Sonia, Sinitta, Marillion and the undisputed worst song ever written: Cliff Richard's *Carrie Doesn't Live Here Anymore.*

I decided to use my alcohol anaesthetic to walk back to the hotel, but nipped into another pub, just opposite and just as grim, called The Boathouse. From the outside it seemed quiet and indeed I was relieved to find that there was no music, so I sat in the corner with my drink. Ten seconds later, out boomed the opening bars of *I've Got a Brand New Combine Harvester* (and I'll Give You The Key), which was then followed by CD2 of the Bad 70s Collection. Clearly the people who run these places think that this is the sort of music which 'strangers' or those from the 'outside world' listen to all the time and they are just trying to be welcoming. The other theory is of course that they are trying to get rid of you.

As I sat reading my book, I felt the eyes of half a dozen men staring at me. These men were not in a group and were not really threatening, although most were quite large and all had tattoos. Every time I looked up, the eyes were there, unflinching, unblinking. I began to fantasise – sorry, that's the wrong word – I began to wonder if I had entered Newburn's gay bar. However, the place did not seem to be one where there would exist a thriving homosexual community, and I think they were probably just curious as to why someone would want to sit down and read in a pub, rather than stand at the bar, drinking slowly, staring into space and saying absolutely nothing to anyone else.

One thing of note about the Boathouse was that it was the only one of the three pubs which did not warn you: 'Do not place cigarette butts into the urinals.' Clearly a big local problem, and one which, judging by the evidence, was in no danger of being overcome.

I hobbled back to the hotel and went to bed, where I immediately fell asleep, only to be woken up by the drunken antics of some fellow guests at around 4am. After that it was hard to get back to sleep again, and worryingly my feet were still aching although there was no pressure on them. When I eventually got up, I covered the blisters in plasters and put on three pairs of socks. These felt quite buffeted now and I was reasonably content as I went down to breakfast.

Breakfast was served by a couple in their

60s, perhaps 70s, and was very good indeed, marred only by the assumption that I would be drinking tea rather than coffee. I detest tea, but in that polite British sort of way, found myself pouring a small amount into the cup to give the impression that I had drunk some, even mixing in a little milk. I then felt rather guilty that the old couple, on seeing the still full teapot, would realise that I had tried a little and refused to drink any more, or worse still, she would pick up the pot imagining it to be emptier and thus spill some of the boiling liquid onto her frail body. I thought about pouring some more down the sink (breakfast was in the bar room). There was no-one else around – the other guests were presumably and hopefully very hung over – so I picked up the teapot and walked towards the bar. The old man entered and I did an about-turn, trying to hide the teapot with my left hand, my fingers splayed out and for some odd reason, waving gently, hoping to hide it. He watched me sit down, his eyes glued to the pot and my idiotically waving hand which partially covered it, no doubt thinking I was trying to steal it. Hide it behind the bar and pick it up later.

'I'm looking forward to the match today, like. See ya later.'

That's all he said, and without waiting for an answer, he was gone, as I was, a few minutes later, from the Newburn Hotel, leaving Newcastle and back up to the route of the Wall, and soon into Northumberland.

3

Newcastle to Corbridge

I didn't consider it cheating. Having walked the day before down the hill from the Wall to Newburn, it was entirely in order, especially with sore feet, however well-padded, to catch a taxi back up there. The driver must have thought I was on speed as, having been starved of any decent conversation for two days, I babbled incessantly for the entire five minute journey, telling him all about my walk, my stay in Newburn, my childhood, my mishap at the careers fair and a thousand and one other things. Soon I was at Heddon-on-the-Wall, where there is another longer stretch of Wall.

Unfortunately the village of Heddon will forever now be linked with the terrible outbreak of foot and mouth disease which devastated so much of the country's farming and tourism industries in 2001. On 19 February of that year an outbreak of the disease, which has a debilitating, though not usually fatal, effect on a number of farm and wild animals, was suspected and later confirmed at a farm in Essex. The procedure for containment is to slaughter and dispose of the animals as quickly as possible, and that farm in Essex lost two cattle and 308 sheep the next day.

Epidemiologists have subsequently traced the origins of the outbreak to a pig-fattening farm near Heddon (where the disease was confirmed on 22 February). A farm four miles from there was also confirmed with the disease and, worryingly, it was believed that its movement through the Wall country had been wind-assisted. The connection with Essex was the livestock which had been sent from Heddon to an abattoir down there.

The spread of the disease and its rapidity makes for a macabre study. Forty sheep from the second Heddon farm were sent to Hexham Market, a few miles away, where they were bought by a Devon farmer. Before travelling back to the West Country, the Devon farmer had made a short stop at Longtown Market, just north of Carlisle. On 21 February (only one day after the confirmation in Essex, and two before that in Heddon), some infected sheep were transported to Wiltshire, Herefordshire and Northampton.

A large part of the country had now been tainted, but despite this, it was the north which suffered most in an outbreak which lasted until the end of September and spread as far as Ireland, Germany, France and the Netherlands. In Essex there were eventually eleven separate confirmed cases; in Northumberland, the total was eighty seven; in County Durham, ninety three; North Yorkshire 135; Dumfries and Galloway 176; and in Cumbria, a heartbreaking 893. By the end of the year, some six and a half million animals had been slaughtered – mainly sheep, but also pigs and cattle and a few goats and deer.

Cumbria was a strange place to live during the spring and summer of 2001. Living in a village to the east of Carlisle, we had to put up with the stench of burning funeral pyres – one of the main methods of carcass disposal. In other places. especially to the west of Carlisle, huge mass burial pits were dug and the bodies bulldozed in and covered up. I remember passing fields on the way to work at the side of the road where sheep and cattle carcasses lay piled up for days awaiting the overstretched services (including the Army which was soon brought in to help out) to take them away for disposal. Schools were closed, sometimes for days where staff and/or pupils were unable to get off the farms where they lived; schools with animals were closed while the animals were slaughtered; other schools, like all farms and a number of shops, had nauseating, disinfectant-soaked carpets placed at the entrances – some are still there today and I saw a few on my walk.

I would not have been able to do my Wall walk a couple of years earlier, as all of the footpaths were closed. Tourism was decimated and there was an inevitable, but still ugly, conflict between the farming community and the tourism industry. The Lake District was largely closed, despite the official line of 'Cumbria – still open for business' and a frightening number of hotels and other business were in danger of going under. The farmers, these people argued, were being compensated for every animal that was slaughtered, but there was no compensation for the much larger tourism industry.

Fell runners had to train by splashing through the sandy shallows of the Solway. Fox hunting was temporarily banned – and this time there were few protests. Arguments raged as to whether the animals needed to be killed to fight this non-fatal disease. People at work would await with horror and anticipation the first trickles of the scent of burning flesh through the office windows. Hysteria broke out in a few places, especially when it was feared at one point that the disease had been passed over to a human – a false alarm in the end.

Those who were most affected by it all of course were the farmers who watched their herds and flocks being piled up in mounds on their land and the farm gates barred from public access. For many, their way of life just suddenly stopped. Some couldn't cope and there have been various reports about mental health issues and suicides. The vets and those whose job was simply to kill the animals all day long must also have suffered terribly. One incident in a slaughterhouse near Carlisle resulted in the death of a member of the wrong species – a human.

In 2002, Bobby Waugh, owner of the pig-fattening farm near Heddon, was found guilty of failing to notify the authorities of the outbreak at his Burnside Farm, and of various other charges including feeding unprocessed waste to animals, failing to properly dispose of animal by-products and of causing unnecessary suffering to pigs. I have spoken with members of the farming community whose opinions are divided. Some see him as the perpetrator of something which has changed their lives forever; others see him as a scapegoat and that others (usually the Government, the NFU, the EU or the consumer demanding cheap food) are to blame.

As I walked through Heddon-on-the-Wall I was reminded of those terrible times and this is unfair to the village. For hundreds of years it has been known mainly because of its association with the Romans, but foot and mouth is a disease which can break out at any time. Hopefully, when it next does, we will have learned a few lessons from 2001.

I turned right and started walking alongside the B6318 which shadows the line of the Wall all the way to the Cumbria-Northumberland border. There is a very good reason for this. This road is known as the Military Road or sometimes Wade's Military Road. It should not be confused with the Roman Military Way which lies between the vallum and the Wall.

In 1745, the Jacobite uprising, which had begun in Scotland under the leadership of the Catholic Bonnie Prince Charlie, crossed the border and reached Carlisle, where the Prince was declared King of the United Kingdom. From there the Jacobites hoped to march down through England and reach London. The march did go considerably further south, as far as Derby, but was ultimately unsuccessful. It is said that the government forces, under General Wade, were unable to move quickly from the north east over to Carlisle to prevent the proclamation, and the government decided to do something about it.

An Act of Parliament was passed initiating the construction of a 'military' road from Newcastle to Carlisle, thus improving east-west mobility. This was in 1753, some five years after the death of Wade, although the road is usually associated with him. The eighteenth century builders unfortunately had little regard for the treasures of antiquity and for most of the distance between Newcastle and Milecastle 33, just before the Wall diverts up the crags, and afterwards near Gilsland, the Wall's foundations were simply absorbed into the road.

This was immediately apparent as I travelled west, away from Heddon, where the Wall ditch could be seen beside me on my right hand side. For some unknown but gracious reason, the hundred metre stretch of Wall in Heddon had been ignored by the engineers. It would be nice to think that they had deliberately left this intact (or rather what is left of it) for posterity, and to give the village some reason for its name.

The Military Road passes over the much busier A69 and thence moves up the hill towards the next fort at Rudchester (which means 'the fort belonging to Rudda', a Scandinavian feminine name). In Roman times the fort was known as Vindovala, which probably means 'white or pleasant high point'. There is now nothing to see, although I could make out the gentle rise of the fort platform. After the building of the Military Road, the fort was ransacked for stone. This was a cavalry fort and it has been partially excavated in the past. In 1953 a temple to the eastern God Mithras was found.

The Romans were remarkably tolerant when it came to religion. As well as worship of the old gods, borrowed from the Greeks, of whom Jupiter (or Jove) was the 'greatest and best' (Optimus Maximus), as the empire spread, a number of local gods were adopted. One of these was the Persian warrior god, Mithras, whose cult was confined exclusively to men of officer rank and offered a happy life to its followers, including secret rites and various stages of initiation. Mithras was said to have captured and slaughtered a bull which had been born at the time of the world's creation and which represented evil. From the dead bull came forth vital life forces which had been contained in its blood. Incidentally, Mithras was born on the 25 December – a date of celebration subsequently borrowed for another religious festival.

The Romans did have issues with two of the main religions: Christianity and Druidism. The problem with Christianity (before the Romans adopted it and spread it throughout the known world) was its intolerance of other religions. Calling itself the one true faith was seen in a similar way as we view racism or sadly, as some religions still surviving may be seen today, including branches of the Christian Church whose intolerance of others has caused no little strife during the past 2,000 years. As regards the native British religions which the Romans found on their arrival, persecution of the human-sacrificing Druidism is more understandable, although the religion may have acted as a focal point of opposition to the occupation.

My feet had now begun to hurt again, quite badly and as well as the blisters, my toes were now being crushed by the extra layers of socks squeezed into my boots. I had had these boots for a couple of years and done numerous walks in them, though not I admit of such a length. As I left Rudchester I had my first poisonous thoughts of giving up, but I pushed on, at a very slow pace of one and a half miles per hour. My spirits were raised as I saw my first fellow walker coming towards me. Perhaps we would sit down together and swap stories? I would be able to rest my feet and have a conversation with someone again. I promised to myself to let the other person also speak this time.

But he said 'hello' and kept walking. The pain in my feet and shoulders, coupled with this rejection, actually brought me close to tears. I had to keep plodding on and began to sing to myself. Being in a field, this brought the attention of a herd of cows who moved rapidly towards me. One cow stood in my path and did not seem to want to let me pass. It was just like when you are in a busy street and face-to-face with someone, you both try to get out of each other's way, but unluckily keep choosing the same direction, until one of you decides to just stand still. With this cow, however, I'm not sure it was accidental. After a while I decided to try and body-swerve past and sell the cow a dummy. However, with my body going one way, and the momentum of my rucksack pulling me the other, I ended up flat on my back, fortunately landing between, and not in, three large cowpats. The thud scared the cows and they scampered off. I began to giggle again, happy that at least the cows had liked my singing.

I began the slow ascent up Harlow Hill to the background buzzing of what I again took to be pylons, except that there were none, and I eventually tracked the noise to the wheat or corn next to me. If anyone can explain this phenomenon I'd be most grateful.

I crossed the Whittledean Reservoirs and made my way painfully towards the Robin Hood pub at East Wallhouses, where I would have a drink, perhaps lunch, and reassess the feet situation. I had just developed a contingency Plan B, which consisted of getting a taxi from the pub into Corbridge, four miles away, (where I had a room booked for the night), buying some new boots, and getting a lift back to the Wall the next day, continuing afresh. For the moment, however, the promise of a rest and an anaesthetic beer was very enticing. I would also be able to get my official Hadrian's Wall passport (which I had picked up at the bed and breakfast in Walls-end) stamped as the pub was the second official stamping station.

I arrived at the Robin Hood at 11.30am and found that, like Jessie Mothersole some eighty years before me, it was closed. Hunter Davies had also had a problem here, though in his case he arrived just too late. He eventually persuaded the landlord to give him a drink. The omens should have been enough for me. I sat down at the side of the road and made a decision to call a taxi and go to Corbridge, justifying this on the grounds of 'well if I walk any further in these boots today, I will not be able to continue this walk afterwards.' Luckily my mobile had a signal and I spent a few seconds deciding which of the forty-odd new '118' numbers to ring, as the old directory inquiries had just gone out of business. With an odd sense of loyalty, I rang the BT number 118 500 and managed to get the number of a Corbridge taxi firm. I rang this number and the guy at the other end said he would be with me in ten minutes.

As I was putting the phone back into my pocket, a taxi pulled up, leaving me confused but delighted at such service. A man got out and came towards me. He was French.

''Ow do I get to Ebchester, please'?'

'Sorry, I don't really know this area,' I said, though I really ought to have got my maps out.

'You are not here?'

'No, I'm walking.'

Both of us then seemed to realise how ludicrous our exchange had been, before he drove off. On the wrong side of the road.

Ten minutes later, my 'real' taxi arrived and four minutes after that I was dropped off at the Roman site just north of Corbridge.

Before the building of the Wall, Corbridge was an important Roman fort at one end of the Stanegate, the Roman road which led to Carlisle. In later times it served as an important supply base for the army in the north. There has been much excavation here and the site, owned by English Heritage, is well worth a visit, even when you feel it would be better to be searching for medical advice about your feet. As I waited to receive my walk-around personal stereo sort-of-thing, a Scottish couple, late fifties/early sixties, were telling the person behind the counter how this was their second visit to the Wall in two weeks. Last week they had walked the entire length, from Wallsend to Bowness. It had taken them four days! Suitably chastened, I left my rucksack in the shop and limped badly around the remains and the museum for the next hour or so.

Among the most famous items to have been found here is the 'Corbridge Lion', a sculpture showing a lion attacking a stag, originally carved as a grave stone, but later used as a fountain, with a hole pierced through the lion's mouth. In 1201, King John, hearing a rumour of buried treasure, authorised some digging at the Roman site, but nothing was found at that time. Later on, the entire contents of an armourer's workshop and 159 gold coins were found.

Both the modern name of the town and the Roman one, Corstopitum, are thought to derive from a local native tribe, the Corio. As well as sitting strategically at one end of the Stanegate, the remains of which can also be seen at the English Heritage site, Corbridge also straddled the important north-south route, known later as Dere Street (from the Anglo-Saxon kingdom of Deira). This road was built around the same time as Corstopitum, beginning at York and going all the way through the north of England and the Scottish borders to the Firth of Forth. There was a series of garrison towns and forts along the way, including Isurium Brigantum (Aldborough), Cataractonium (Catterick), Morbium (Piercebridge), Vinovia (Binchester), Longovicium (Lanchester), Vindomora (Ebchester – I wonder if the French taxi-driver ever made it?), Corstopitum (Corbridge), and Bremenium (Rochester). The road crossed the wall at Portgate, just a couple of miles north of Corbridge where the modern A68 does the same.

I left the Roman site and began the slow and painful half-mile walk down into the town, hoping that a bus would perhaps pass me or a car full of professional Swedish foot-masseuses would stop and pick me up and take me back to their caravan and...

With delirious fantasies like this to fill the time, I managed to make it into town and walked through, looking for an outdoor shop which might sell top-of-the-range-don't-care-how-much-they-cost walking boots. A few minutes later I realised that I was heading out of town, south towards the river. Across the magnificent traffic-controlled bridge lay the bed and breakfast, where I had booked a room for the night, and the train station. Coincidentally, for the third consecutive night, I would be staying in a Station Road. I actually passed the B&B but continued for a little while towards the station, to check out train times to Hexham, the nearest big town, which was bound to have an appropriate shop. There was a train in half an hour and a return train an hour after that, so I sat down, opened a bag of salted peanuts, realising immediately how hungry I had been.

Hexham's history dates back to the founding of the Abbey by St Wilfred in 671 AD and since then the town has been an important ecclesiastical centre. The market began in the thirteenth century and after that tanning, glove and hat making became the major industries for a while. It also claims to have the earliest recorded purpose-built gaol in England, built in 1330 under the auspices of the Archbishop of York. This gaol still stands and now also houses the Border Museum.

The train journey took four minutes and I made for the Tourist Information Office, nervous with anticipation, having put all of my faith in this place. A kind young man confirmed that there was such a shop, and only two minutes walk away, a distance which I somehow managed in around thirty seconds.

Hexham is not of Roman origin, although much of it was built out of pilfered materials from Corstopitum. In the seventh century, St Wilfred built the abbey, which still dominates the town, and which also houses some

Roman remains. One of these is a Roman stone, bearing the names of the Emperor Septimius Severus, and his two sons, Caracalla and Geta. Caracalla was one of the madder Roman emperors (sharing the same historical reputation with such names as Caligula and Nero) and to ensure that he and he alone became absolute ruler, he had his brother murdered, a year after Severus died. The Roman stone in Hexham Abbey bears witness to this and Geta's name has been partially erased from it, presumably after his death and on the orders of his brother. I saw none of this and have got the information from a number of books written about the town, although I have subsequently been back there. On that sunny Saturday afternoon, I had a specific time-limited task and had no other objective in mind. I was a Roman soldier marching up Dere Street to patch up the Wall which had been bruised and blistered by the constant pounding of the enemy. I was Mithras in search of a bull to kill. I was a modern day vet rushing to stop the spread of an agricultural epidemic throughout the country. I was clearly some-one who should have eaten more than a bag of salted peanuts in the past seven hours.

I had been directed to one of those large

'retail parks', where designer goods are sold at discount prices, and once inside made straight for the outdoor place and quickly bought the most comfortable (but not most expensive) boots in the shop. Trying them on, the difference was immediate and heartbreakingly wonderful. For the second time that day I was actually close to tears. The young man who served me was extremely helpful, although knowing that he had a 100% chance of a sale must have helped. He told me that if I tried on the boots later tonight and wore them for a bit without going outside, I could always bring them back and change them if they weren't quite right. However we both knew that as soon as I got out of the shop I would be ripping off my old shoes again and discarding them in favour of the new ones. In fact I actually lasted until I got back to Corbridge, as I realised that I had spent longer than I'd thought in the shop, trying on different sorts of orgasmic boots and shoes, and had to make a painful dash to the station.

Back in Corbridge I made for Fellcroft, the bed and breakfast, had a shower, got changed and devoured the complimentary chocolate biscuits whilst checking the football results. Everyone that day, including the old man at breakfast in Newburn eyeing me and the teapot suspiciously and the two taxi drivers, had been talking about the Newcastle v Man Utd game, but I was checking for the Carlisle Utd result. They lost 2-0, both goals iron-ically scored by someone with the surname Carlisle. I'm not an avid fan, but I do follow the results and go to the occasional game, where I inevitably enjoy the metamorphosis of my mild and gentle work colleagues into foul-mouthed and rather passionate animals, more than the game itself. As I sat on the bed wolfing down the biscuits, I felt pleased with my day and now more confident that I could continue the walk. That confidence was soon to be bolstered even more by rather too much alcohol.

I first went to the Dyvels, just a few yards down the road from Fellcroft, which had a nice beer garden, where I sat drinking my first beer of the day. At the table next to me were two couples – also 'not from round here', as evidenced by their accents. They at-tracted the attention of one of the friendly but completely pissed locals who began to tell them of his fear that his girlfriend was going to ask for his hand in marriage and that was why he was drunk because he didn't know what his answer would be. 'It'll just come oot ma mooth, like, and, y'knaw, that'll be it and whatever ah've said, well, that'll be ma answer right except that it might no and' ah'll no' know what ah've said and, like, what ma answer has been. Like?' said to the obvious incomprehension of his new friends. After ten or so minutes of this, he suddenly asked them where they came from. It was Somerset.

'Somerset? Somerset? You're joking? Christ Almighty! Honest to God? Somerset? What ya doing up here?'

The anaesthetic alcohol had worked and, with my new boots, I now had enough confidence to walk again, so I set off, back over the bridge into town. Suddenly, with a beautiful orange sun low along the river, Corbridge seemed a much nicer little town than it had a few hours earlier. There was less of an industrial past hanging around the place, as there had been at Wallsend and Newcastle, and would appear at later stops too. There was however evidence of troubled border times in such buildings as the obviously fortified vicarage. This area is now one of the most peaceful and, in places, remote in England, yet the Wall, and the mark of division which it made, started a long series of border skirmishes and border wars – indeed started the idea of a 'border' itself – which lasted for over 1700 years. But more of that later.

I moved now at a fairly lively pace, checking out (by sight only at this point) the various pubs and eating places, walking right through the town. Eventually I stopped at the Wheatsheaf where I ordered a drink and read the menu. It was now nearly six o'clock and realising that they were about to change to the evening menu (i.e. same food, but with 50% mark up on lunchtime prices), I ordered haddock and chips. And, to celebrate my newly found determination to finish the walk, a bottle of house white. The food was deliciously bizarre. The fish and chips came on a bed of water melon, and as a side dish there was a tomato-pasta sort of sauce, but without the pasta. Heavy on the garlic and chillies, so a winner with me. I read the *Guardian* as I ate and as the sun went down and the evening became cooler, the wine kept me warm.

It was still early as I made my way back through the town, so I popped into the Blue Cow for a pint of bitter. As with the two other pubs I visited, the place was full of older people, like myself, in their thirties or even older. Presumably, I remember thinking, the youth are bussed/trained out to Hexham for the night rather than stay in this sleepy little market town. There was a small Co-op/Spar thing nearby so on what was now my way back to the bed and breakfast, I popped in to get some water, some chocolate, oh and a half bottle of whisky which I convinced myself also counted as emergency rations and purely for medicinal purposes. Next door was another pub, the Golden Lion, where Harrison had stayed in 1956. I'm not sure he would have approved of the place these days as it was here where I found the town's under-30s, listening to the in-house disco playing a souped-up version of Boney M. No doubt had I stayed longer I would have heard gangsta-rap versions of the Wurzels, but I took my leave and not just because four middle-aged people had entered the pub, looked around confusingly and in awe at the naked teenage flesh grinding away, and decided to join me at my table. It was now definitely time to call it a night.

So I stopped for one last pint at the Angel Inn, before crossing the bridge, passing my bed and breakfast and visiting the Dyvels for the second time that day. I had one last beer (it was the last this time) and drunkenly began texting loads of people. Suddenly feeling guilty about the amount of money I had spent that day (two taxis, £90 boots, lots of food and alcohol), I decided to take the opportunity presented by sitting in an empty beer garden in the dark, and began to drink my whisky.

I arrived back at Fellcroft around 10.30pm and was asleep five minutes later.

Next morning, unsurprisingly I woke with a bit of a heavy head, which was helped only marginally by a wonderful shower. My room was not en-suite, but I did have the sole use of one of the bathrooms. Before breakfast, I packed my rucksack, having now to contend with an extra pair of boots (I just couldn't bring myself to discard them) and a half-empty half bottle of Jamiesons. The act of leaving my razor in Wallsend, in an attempt to lighten my baggage, was now proved entirely futile and, worryingly, I began giggling again, this time finding it quite difficult to stop.

Downstairs in the breakfast room, the table was set for three, and the Sunday papers were available for perusal. I was soon joined by a couple from Lincoln who had relatives in the area (he was originally from Prudhoe, just down the road) and were up visiting for the weekend. The owners were a very genial couple, the Browns. He was local, hailing from Wallsend. She came from Oslo and was pleasantly chatty. The breakfast was the best I ate all week – and they offered me more, but I had already eaten enough for about five people. It also did the trick with the hangover.

But better things were still to come in the way of a lift back up to the Roman Wall, thus saving me three miles or so which would have been dull and again was not part of the Wall walk. As he drove, Mr Brown mentioned how the opening of the trail had definitely led to an increase in business. I was sad to leave Corbridge, not just because of my hedonistic night on the piss or because of the wonderful hospitality at the bed and breakfast, but I was also looking forward to walking the Wall again, hopefully without too much pain.

4

Corbridge to Newbrough

I still didn't consider it cheating. But I had missed some of the Wall route, so had to make a quick detour back eastwards, before being able to continue my proper journey.

On this detour I passed the site of the fifth fort on the Wall, at Haltonchesters. The Roman name was Onnum, which derives from the Celtic word for water. A stream runs next to the Wall here. I also passed over the ancient Portgate, now the roundabout intersection of the Military Road and Dere Street.

The sun was rising and I was determined this was going to be a good day without foot problems. I began to see many more other walkers now too, although sadly, most of them did seem to be having problems and some were walking in obvious distress. I felt like an old hand now and approached a few with words of concern and trying to give the impression that I was Britain's best chiropodist.

Roman rule in Britain lasted around four hundred years beginning with the invasions ordered by the emperor Claudius in 43AD. The previous invasions some hundred years earlier by Julius Caesar do not really count. Julius came and saw, but did not conquer. Hadrian visited in 122, and decided to build the Wall and a number of other forts in the area, including that at Bewcastle (Fanum Cocidii, the altar of the native god Cocidius). The next emperor, Antoninus Pius, decided to push the 'border' further north and built another Wall, entirely made of turf but with more forts along the way, between the Forth and Clyde. Had this Wall endured, perhaps Edinburgh and Glasgow would now be border cities, but as it happens, it was abandoned after around thirty years and Hadrian's Wall became the frontier once again.

Around 180AD, there is evidence of an attack on the Wall by northern tribes and of damage to a number of the forts including Vindobala, Onnum, Corstopitum and Banna (Birdoswald) on the Wall. There was also damage to some of the outpost forts, such as Risingham, which were not then rebuilt. In 197, the emperor Commodus was assassinated and one of the claimants to the throne was Clodius Albinus, the governor of Britain. At one point it is thought that in his pursuit of power he took some of the Wall garrison across the channel to fight and this led to serious destruction of the undefended frontier. However, it is possible that this destruction came a few years later, around 205. For whatever reason, destruction there certainly was and the eventual winner of the imperial purple, Septimius Severus, came to Britain, with his sons Caracalla and Geta, and began a clean-up/wipe-out operation of the northern tribes. When Severus died at York in 211, his two sons made peace with the tribes and returned to Rome, leaving Britain at the start of a century of peace, although, as we have seen, willing to fight each other.

The outpost forts at Netherby, Bewcastle, Risingham and High Rochester were now re-built and it seems that Roman rule, or at least 'protection' extended far into the Scottish border area. The peaceful times led to a reduction in the Wall garrison and even the lack of maintenance at several Wall forts, particularly Onnum and Banna. By the early 300s, there was increasing trouble from the Picts. In 343, the emperor Constans came to Britain and throughout the 360s the Picts became more and more of an issue. In 367, the 'Barbarian Conspiracy' of Picts, Scots, Saxons, Franks and Atacotti was eventually put down by the strangely medieval sounding, but very Roman, Count Theodosius. The outpost forts were finally abandoned forever.

In 383, the Roman army in Britain was taken over the Channel by Magnus Maximus for use in more civil war type of fighting, and whether it returned or not, the army was eventually called back to Rome to help in dealing with attacks there. In 410, Rome was attacked by the Visigoths and the Emperor Honorius gave an indication of the new foreign policy by telling those in Britannia simply to 'defend yourselves' against any attacks from the new kids on the block, the Anglo-Saxon raiders, hailing from Germany. By 426, the Romans had totally abandoned Britain and a final plea for assistance in 446 did not even receive a response.

Well, that is one view of the abandonment of Britain by the Romans – and probably the prevailing one. There are, as usual, other theories.

Keep in mind that by the early fifth century the vast majority of auxiliaries would have been recruited in Britain and certainly not in Rome. As part of an army, they would of course have followed the orders of their commanders, but few would have had any affinity or loyalty to Italy.

There was a major invasion of Britain in 408 and because the 'Roman' army failed to deal with it properly, the civilians were forced into setting up their own defences – the first 'Dad's Army', if you like. Perhaps the Britons simply got fed up with this increasingly inefficient and expensive force and gradually took over the government with little resistance from the Emperor? Perhaps.

Whatever actually happened and why will never be known. What is clear is that the native Britons continued for some time to follow Roman customs and administrative practices, even after the arrival of the Anglo-Saxons.

Anglo-Saxon is a name given to three groups of people: Angles, Saxons and Jutes who had been operating in the south east of England during the final years of Roman rule. With the Romans gone, they began to conquer the island. Kent fell first and then Anglo-Saxon kingdoms were set up in Essex, Middlesex, Wessex and Sussex. There were also kingdoms in East Anglia and North-umbria, leaving Britannia split into different territories each ruled by a king. A number of Britons fled to Wales and some fought the invaders. One of the most famous native British rebels was of course King Arthur who was from Wales or Cumbria or Cornwall, depending on your point of view. Having fled to Wales, he is believed to have used Roman cavalry tactics on the Anglo-Saxons and after a relatively successful career was finally killed in 537AD. Many of the myths surrounding this king however, including the Round Table, Guinevere, Lancelot and Excalibur did not emerge until over 500 years later.

The most powerful Anglo-Saxon kingdoms were Wessex, Mercia (in the midlands), and Northumbria. This latter kingdom brought together two smaller provinces, Bernicia and Deira, in the early 600s and covered the eastern area of Hadrian's Wall, going as far south as the Humber, and north to the Forth. In the west, covering Cumbria and across the modern border, was the British Kingdom of Rheged, although this was eventually swallowed by Northumbria some time around the middle of the seventh century. Incidentally, the big three of Wessex, Mercia and Northumbria swallowed up the rest of England between them. Then the Vikings invaded some time before 800AD, gradually taking control of most of the country. The Kingdom of Wessex, led by the Saxon, Alfred the Great was, in time, the only credible opposition to the Scandinavians and Alfred defeated them at the battle of Athelney in 878 and again in Wiltshire the next year. In 886, Alfred captured London and he was effectively recognised by the Vikings as King of Wessex. The country was now split between Wessex and Danelaw, the Viking part. This arrangement more or less remained (though not peacefully between the two) until William the Conqueror arrived in 1066.

So there you have a very threadbare summary of the history of England during the first millennium AD, written here simply to put into context some of the things I would see while walking along the Wall.

The next few miles, from Portgate westwards, made for a pleasant country walk, following the path which is mostly off-road, but just next to it. For a lot of the way, the ditch to the north and the vallum to the south were visible, confirming that the road had been built right on top of the Wall. Somewhere just after the site of Milecastle 25 (again a good indication of how far I had travelled), I saw a church in the field to my right and to my left, at the side of the road, a large wooden cross. Here, in 634, King Oswald of the Anglo-Saxon kingdom of Northumbria defeated the Celtic King Cadwallon of Gwynedd. This decisive battle has been turned into both a victory for Anglo-Saxons over Celts, and also of Christianity over Paganism (although Cadwallon was also a Christian). In Bede's day (672-735), the site, known as Heofenfeld, or Heaven Field, was: 'held in much veneration, where Oswald, when he was about to engage in battle, set up the sign of the Holy Cross, and on his knees prayed to God that he would send heavenly aid to His worshippers in their dire need.' God answered his prayers and a church was built on the spot in memory of the battle. Both the current church and the cross are much more recent, being built in 1737 and 'in the 1930s', (according to a sign set up beside the cross) respectively. Oswald was later canonised, as Bede says, in repayment for setting up his Holy Cross as before that: 'there was no sign of the Christian faith, no church, no altar erected throughout all the nation of the Bernicians', one of the two kingdoms which had combined to form Northumbria.

Later on, back at home reading Bede, I found out that: 'innumerable miracles of healing are known to have been wrought in the place... And even to this day, many people are in the habit of cutting splinters from the wood of this holy cross and putting them in water which they then give to sick men or beasts to drink or else they sprinkle them with it; and they are quickly restored to health.' I should have broken off a piece of the cross, soaked it in my drinking water and stuffed it down my socks.

A little further on, in a field opposite, I

came across a rather spectacular piece of Wall. This is at Planetrees and is interesting for two reasons. Firstly, this seems to be the exact place where the Wall, narrow from Wallsend to Newcastle, and then broad from there, becomes narrow again. The foundations, having been built slightly earlier, remain broad. Secondly, local legend has it that this stretch of Wall was preserved as a result of the entreaties of old William Hutton, who, when walking here in 1801, came across its piecemeal destruction. 'The proprietor,' he wrote, 'is now taking it down to erect a farm-house with the materials... I desired the servant with whom I conversed to give my compliments to Mr Tulip (the proprietor), and request him to desist, or he would wound the whole body of Antiquaries. As he was putting an end to the most notable monument of Antiquity in the whole island, they would feel every stroke.'

Faced with such threats and beseeching, or perhaps maybe he had enough stone already, or, then again, perhaps realising the importance of this particular stretch, Mr Tulip did not demolish all of the Wall, leaving this little bit for us to look at.

The official trail takes you away from the Wall at this point, and, although shown differently in the guidebook, right up to the outskirts of the village of Wall, before going back down the road towards Chollerford. To the east is the River North Tyne and on the other side, I could make out the fort of Chesters, where large crowds were gathering, cars were parking and from where the muffled sounds from a tannoy were being carried in the wind. To the right is Brunton Turret (26b), which is relatively well preserved.

Coming down into Chollerford, just before crossing the bridge, I followed a sign directing me down the riverside towards the remains of the Roman Bridge. The walk there seemed to take ages and I was desperate to get round to the fort and sort out another physical problem I was having. But more of that in a minute. The bridge remains were eventually worth seeing. The abutment on the west side (the fort side) is now under water, as the river has moved over the centuries, but this means the eastern abutment is accessible. A bridge was built here originally at the time of the Wall and the Wall 'passed over' it, before linking to the fort. This Hadrianic bridge was a smaller affair than the remains suggest, and a larger bridge was built under Severus. I was joined by a young couple who in between arguing about which bits were Severan and which Hadrianic, were giggling at a large penis, which had been carved into the stones by the Romans. Modern opinion seems to hold that such carvings were not obscene gestures, but a device to ward off evil and bring good luck. I wish I had known that in my second year at high school when I was reprimanded by my music teacher for drawing a similar anatomical symbol on the inside cover of my homework diary, complete with the music teacher's name and an arrow linking the two. 'But Sir, in the best Roman tradition, I am simply wishing you good luck!'

Across the water, Chesters fort, originally known as Cilurnum ('large pool'), lay only a few metres away. However to get there I needed to walk back up to the modern bridge, built in 1775, over it and down the other river bank, a journey of at least another mile. It was a hot Sunday morning, I was hungry, thirsty and sweating and my thighs were rubbing against my combat-type shorts, so I was hoping to buy some cream or a bandage or something at the garage in town or perhaps there would be a mini-shop at the fort itself. The garage, alas, sold nothing but fuel, chocolate and 'internet access'. Why anyone would come all the way out here to surf the web is a question worth asking. Maybe it has the only decent connection in miles? Maybe it's for the in-store entertainment for the lonely employees out of season.

I arrived at the fort, to find out that there was an 'event' taking place, one of those re-enactment groups which I thoroughly enjoy, though can't admit to in a non-historical environment. It's the sort of thing I often go to at Carlisle Castle and bump into work colleagues who try and avoid my eye. At this event, which was lasting for two days (it was the August bank holiday weekend), there were soldiers, cavalry and a sort of Roman-times village, a vicus. These 'vici' sprang up alongside and to the south of the Wall, providing all sorts of services – inns, shops, brothels – for the garrison, who would spend their wages here.

Naturally, attachments and relationships formed, although before the third century, Roman soldiers could not legally marry. Many however went through some sort of local ceremony and therefore there were a number of unofficial wives, and inevitably, children. When the soldier was discharged, after his twenty five years of service (and sixty per cent of them survived to this), any children born from this 'wedlock', became citizens along with their father. Until then the children, indeed the wife, had no legal status and could be abandoned at any time, especially if the unit was moved elsewhere.

Initially each vicus was built on the other side (south) of the Valium, and therefore outside the military area. After time, however, the settlements tended to creep over the Vallum and closer to the fort.

I watched the cavalry display where the crowd was encouraged to cheer for one of the three horsemen: Maximus (the strong and gorgeous Roman), Brittanicus (the underdog, the local hero) and Germanicus (the obvious buffoon with a beard, stereotyped to the point of no return – he had no sense of humour). One of the young kids in front of me, got over excited and wet himself. Next to him, another one shouted out in his London brogue, 'Come on Maximus, knock 'is fahkin' 'ead orff.' His mother went to slap him around the ears, but he ducked and she hit the (non-related) other kid instead, the one who had pissed himself. The horseback fight in front of us was play-acting, but a real one between two sunburnt mothers seemed about to take place, much to the crowd's delight. But the 'wronged' mother noticed her child's wet shorts and marched him off and the tension dissipated.

The fort itself is one of the better and more interesting sights on the Wall and there is also a museum there, largely made up of the private collection of John Clayton who began to excavate the fort – which he owned, along with Carrawburgh, Housesteads and Vindolanda – in the 1830s. Roman forts were pretty much standard in their design – it is usually said that the idea was that a Roman soldier from any part of the empire would be able to find his way around any Roman fort, wherever it was. This is maybe a bit simplistic. The real reason is probably that there are only a limited number of ways in which to fit the required buildings – headquarters, commanding officer's house, granaries, barracks, hospital, ovens, toilets and stables (if necessary) – into the fort. Generally the forts were a playing card shape, but this was adapted where necessary, for example at Bewcastle, where the fort was hexagonal. All the guidebooks mention that forts varied in size from 2 acres (0.8ha) to 9.3 acres (3.7ha). This may mean nothing to you (it didn't to me). Another way of putting it is to say that the smallest fort was around 130m by 130m, and the largest 590m x 590m. Chesters is 5.8 acres (2.3ha) and, as a cavalry fort, did contain extensive stables.

Underneath the fort somewhere lie the remains of Turret 27a. The Wall had already been built when it was decided to put a fort here. Back down towards the river, and just outside the fort, are the remains of the bath house, complete with changing room and the various hot, warm and cold rooms, used in turn by the Romans.

As here at Chesters, the baths tended to be built outside the fort (not sure why: was it as simple a reason as being a fire risk?), but later forts had an internal one. The commanding officer's residence inside Chesters also had a mini bath house built in to it. Furnaces burnt charcoal to produce dry heat or wood for moist heat, essentially giving the soldiers a choice of sauna or Turkish bath. Boilers were made of bronze or lead and the hot air circulated under the floor, which was raised on pillars, and also up through cavities in the wall. The principle is the same as modern central heating systems – except of course that hot air, and not water, was the main instrument.

There were different rooms at different temperatures and also hot and cold baths. There was probably a sequence – moving through successively warmer stages until reaching the hot bath – although it is quite possible that there were some madmen who plunged straight into the cold bath. However, certainly at Chesters, the warm and hot rooms outnumber the colder ones. Oil was used, rubbed into the skin and scraped off, rather than soap, and there was also a masseur on hand to pummel your back and slap your thighs.

As well as its cleansing properties, the bath house also had a place in the social life of the Romans, although men and women were supposed to go at different times, unless separate (and usually inferior) facilities had been provided for women. A number of Roman writers have left details about their institutional importance. Those at the Roman city of Aquae Sulis in south west England are still an impressive tourist attraction. That particular city has grown since then and its name is now, appropriately, simply, Bath.

There is a small café at the fort, and a shop – Lucullus' Larder, named after the 1st century BC Consul whose wealth and riches are now universally applied as an epithet to good food. I was able to buy a sandwich and sit in the sun eating it, but could find nothing obvious which would alleviate the pain caused by the friction between shorts and legs. I desperately needed something, as I still had another three miles to walk that day, and decided upon a small jar of English Heritage strawberry lip balm. Once outside the fort, I found a quiet spot in the car park, just round the back from the main ticket office and between what I took to be workmen's huts. Carefully ensuring that no-one was looking, I delved out a large dollop of the balm and put one hand down the front of my (now unbuttoned) shorts and the other up the right leg and began to rub the fragrant wax around my thighs. The stinging pain was indescribable. I gave out an involuntary yelp, looked up and saw two old women, staring at me in disbelief. 'Lip balm. Sore thighs,' I tried to explain, but they hurried away, no doubt to call one of the security guards. The stinging subsided and once this had gone I realised that the lip balm actually worked. I quickly repeated the procedure with the other leg, being spotted once again by a very attractive teenage girl who, I swear, smiled wickedly at me. She, like the older ladies, had been visiting the workmen's huts, which I discovered were actually portaloos.

Thus repaired, I hurried off out of the car park, before the security guards came after me. I headed off towards Newbrough, where

I had booked in at Newbrough Park, once a sort of manor house, now a bed and breakfast. This meant a three mile walk south and away from the Wall, down and uphill. It was a nice country walk and it was good to get away from the crowds again, back into a bit of solitude. About a mile from Newbrough, I came to the village of Fourstones, apparently named so because it is four miles from Hexham. There was a pub here, The Railway Inn (I just couldn't get away from things to do with trains), and as I was thirsty I decided to investigate. The pub was reasonably crowded (it was just after 3pm and lunch had finished being served), but I found a stool at the bar, which I sat on, before immediately losing my balance and falling off backwards onto the floor. Four faces peered down at me. 'You want to take that rucksack off, sir. Are you OK?'

I was fine, just a little embarrassed, and tried to shrink behind my glass of water and bottle of beer. I got talking to a couple of friendly guys who asked how far I had walked (around ten miles that day), where I was staying and so on.

'Newbrough Park? Bloody hell. Bet that's a bit pricey? You'll be getting breakfast with steel cutlery,' he said. I wasn't sure what he meant by this. Was this so unusual? Do Northumbrians use plastic utensils at the first meal of the day? I didn't pursue this but asked about Newbrough itself.

'There's a pub there, the Red Lion, but it's a bit rough. You're better off coming back here, although neither do any food in the evening. Oh look out, here come the Red Lion brigade. That pub closes at 3pm, so they'll have walked here.'

Actually it looked as if they had come on motorbikes, as most of them were wearing leather and two had helmets on (but I noticed there were no bikes outside, when I left). They all looked a bit too old to be dangerous and all were extremely drunk, but quietly so. One who wasn't wearing leather looked like an intoxicated wizard – long thin face, long thin hair, long thin beard, cloak.

'You should come to Pete's BBQ,' said the guy at the bar.

'Yeah everyone else seems to be,' grumbled the other one, who I presume was Pete.

'Oh it'll be fine,' continued the first guy nodding over at the new arrivals, 'at least we'll get away from Merlin and the Hell's Angels.'

A few minutes later, I continued my trek towards Newbrough, passing a garage, the village school, the 'bit rough' Red Lion and arrived at the entrance to Newbrough Park. I knocked on the door and my spirits fell when I heard the manic barking of a dog.

The owners were not prepared for me – it was around 4.30pm – and they were still painting my room! I am normally quite wary of dogs, but the resident canine was clearly not going to be a problem and looked incredibly old. In fact, she was only five (or thirty five in human terms – about the same as me!). She staggered around. Perhaps she had been drinking the paint.

This was an old manor house, the current owners having bought it two years ago and turning into a bed and breakfast (rather than a hotel 'for tax purposes'). It was huge inside and the bedroom looked to be very comfortable. I decided I was going to try and enjoy this, for the following two evenings were going to be spent in youth hostels.

I had a shower and a short rest, before rubbing some more strawberry lip balm into my thighs and getting dressed. Walking back into Fourstones, I passed Pete's BBQ, which was spilling onto the main street, but could not see either of the two guys I had met earlier. I hurried on, wanting to get to the garage before 7pm, when it closed. I bought some more plasters (my feet were still a potential issue, but the new boots were heavenly), some crisps, a couple of sausage rolls, some water and a chocolate bar. They had sold out of bread and the last two sandwiches were 'ham and pease pudding'. I have no idea what pease pudding is so I gave it a miss.

Back at the Railway Inn again, the place was much quieter, although Merlin and his mates were still there, playing cards. I found out that the next pub was at Warden, two miles away, where there was no guarantee of food, so decided to stay here for a couple of drinks and head back to Newbrough with my 'picnic'. I could always wash it down with the remainder of my whisky.

I read some more of my books while I drank and ate peanuts. I also arranged to meet Jo and Rufus – my wife and son – next day for lunch at Housesteads, as they were travelling over to the north east. Merlin's circle began to get a bit rowdy and they were warned by the bar staff a few times, before they decided to call it a day, after nine hours of solid drinking.

I stayed for a couple of hours before setting off back towards Newbrough. I heard a shout from behind me, 'You got skis as well, mate?' It was a friendly shout, from someone who had also just left the pub (he was referring to my stick) and we chatted as we walked. He knew quite a bit about local history, telling me that the name New-brough meant 'new fort', and indeed there had been a Roman fort here, on the Stanegate, the line of which I presumed we were walking. But no, the actual line was just to the north of us, in the field. It didn't reach the road until we came to the pub, where he was heading and where I decided to chance it too. He pointed out the indent-ation or mound left by the Roman road, but I could see nothing. He told me he had often thought about buying a metal detector as there was so much buried treasure wait-ing to be uncovered. After that his historical analysis became a bit ropey.

'There were hundreds of forts in this area. See that farm up there? That was one. Iron Age. The school? Stone Age. In the field? Roman. The landlords knocked them down and made off with all the treasure.'

When we got into the pub, I was expecting the conversation to continue, but he immedi-ately disowned me and joined some fellow drunks at the bar, in which were about half a dozen serious drinkers. In the corner, Merlin was asleep. The bitter was repulsive and I gulped down half of it, before giving up. No-one had spoken to me during my short stay, but everyone seemed eager that I was off and wished me good night.

Back at Newbrough Park, I tried to haggle with the owners to get breakfast at 7.30 (as I had a long way to go before my arranged lunchtime rendezvous) and we eventually agreed on 7.45am. However, I was promised a lift back up to the Wall, back to where I had left it.

I ate my sausage rolls, but was asleep within minutes. Breakfast was served at one end of a mile-long table, surrounded by photos of the owners and various public dignitaries. There was an excessive choice of 'starters' – dried fruit, nuts, etc, and of expensive looking jams and marmalades, but the main Northumbrian breakfast (why, not just here, but why – always – the guilty nod towards health with the boiled plum tomato?) was less tasty and cost more than elsewhere.

However, the owners were very friendly people and partially redeemed the deal by driving me back up to Chollerford. In the car, I became aware of the pungent strawberry lip balm emanating from my thighs (I was now thoroughly enjoying the act of application, aware that the not unpleasant warm stinging would soon be replaced by a waxy soothing). I am sure that my driver was aware too, as she kept looking at my lips, presumably trying to see it there. Like others, she told me that with the opening of the Trail, business had really boomed in the past few weeks, although I had been left with the impression – perhaps unfairly – that I had been their first guest ever, their guinea pig. Certainly I am not sure if they are aware how far their voices travel in that cavernous house, as I was treated to some entertaining (but by no means horrible, and in some senses quite touching) dialogue they were holding a few rooms away, down a long corridor. It involved underwear. I am saying nothing more. They were nice people.

5

Newbrough to Once Brewed

Back on the Wall again, the day had started overcast, which was a relief from the hot sun of yesterday and I made good progress. The strawberry balm was doing its job, the boots theirs and I was enjoying the walk. I passed Walwick, meaning 'farm on the Wall' and Black Carts ('carts' = sterile, stony soil'), with a substantial section of Wall, and arrived at Limestone Corner, the northernmost part of the Wall. Here, Harrison was overcome with emotion: 'One achieves that exhilarating certainty that all earth and all heaven are at one's command, that one has made this particular piece of country one's own.' One suspects that one had been snacking on the various fungi to be seen along the way. Or eating his strawberry lip balm.

Here the Vallum can be seen to the south of the road but the northern ditch is incomplete. There are huge blocks of stone scattered around, having been broken off the rock by the Roman builders. Holes had been inserted into the rock and water poured in to soften the rocks in preparation for quarrying, but even this did not always work and so the ditch remains full of these large blocks, cast aside when the soldier-builders gave in.

I soon came to the next fort on the Wall, Brocolitia (Carrawburgh), which originally meant either 'rocky spot', 'heathery spot' or 'place with badgers' depending on who you believe. This is situated just past the site of milecastle 31. The fort was one of the later additions, and was built on top of the Vallum, probably around 130AD. There isn't much to see of the fort itself, but there are two other items of interest.

The first is the Well of Coventina which again cannot be seen. As with modern-day fountains, this was a place where the Romans had chucked their coins, hoping for good luck. 13,487 were found in 1876, with most disappearing immediately, after news of the find had spread. Coventina was a local deity, a water nymph. She may have been Celtic, a local, adopted by the soldiers, but then again, she may have been Greek and brought over by them. Despite not being recorded anywhere else in the Empire, she must have had some local status to have received such a large number of coins. The well appears to have suffered a violent end but we can only conjecture what actually happened. In 1879, Collingwood Bruce arranged for the coins – most of which he eventually managed to recover – to be melted down and cast into an eagle weighing 6.5kg.

The second feature is the Mithraic Temple, a replica of which I had seen in the New-castle Museum. There is a car park on the southern side of the road, and this had been full, when I had arrived, but, apart from a chain-smoking American, there was no-one else to be seen. As I made my way down to the remains of the Temple, the legacy of four consecutive cooked breakfasts and a sudden visual shock almost combined in cardiac arrest. Over the brow of the hill came about thirty Roman soldiers, with 'wives' and kids. I could hear an involuntary whine coming from somewhere about my person and was about to run for cover, when I came to my senses and realised they were clearly the same re-enactment society who had been at Chesters the day before and were probably on their way back now (it being a Bank Holiday Monday). As I got closer a number of them were swinging their car keys which seemed rather incongruous and, although they were off-duty (but dressed-up), I noticed that the men just could not help themselves from walking in step. The Romans allegedly shouted out, 'Sin... Sin... Sin-Dex-Sin', in the same way we (well, those who march) go 'Left... Left... Left-Right-Left'. The full words were 'sinister' (left) and 'dexter' (right). As with some more modern cultures, left-handed people were considered rather dubious.

Down at the Temple, a group of the 'soldiers' were arguing. I realised that a number of re-enactment societies were involved, as one small and rotund man was stabbing his finger at another much more handsome and clearly vain guy, 'Well, your lot advertise yourselves as coming from the time of Augustus down to Hadrian, but most of your stuff is so obviously from the time of Claudius and Nero.'

The handsome guy responded, 'And you have hardly any pre-Flavian armour.'

There was an audible gasp from the crowd. This was clearly below the belt. Someone intervened before it came to blows.

'Listen, you two, nobody's perfect. I mean, I wear a dagger and there is evidence that after 70AD, the army did not use daggers.' This did not help. The others approached him with murmurs of, 'Do you?' and 'Really? You wear a dagger?' and began lifting up his tunic. I thought about telling them, in Latin of course, to shut up and that I wanted to be at peace here in the Temple with my god, but chickened out and made my way across the field and back to the line of the Wall.

For the next three miles the Wall runs alongside the road, but then the two separate and while this is pleasant, the terrain becomes much rougher and tougher. The first of the five loughs (lakes) can be seen just south of the line, at Shield on the Wall. In Roman times, the area was full of mini-loughs and was real fen-land. Basins had been moulded out of the rock during the Ice Age creating small nutrient-rich pools which were devoured by reeds. Eventually moss covered most of the loughs.

The area of the Wall can be split into five main geological sections. The first, again, going east to west, is the coalfield, laid down in the Carboniferous period (300 million years ago). This was shaped by the Ice Age glaciers which levelled the land, leaving clay, sand and gravel and no real problems for the Roman builders.

The second area, starting around Heddon-on-the-Wall, sees limestone, formed when the land was covered by sea and the remains of sea creatures were compacted together on the sea bed. Limestone was burned in kilns to make lime mortar for the Wall, especially under Severus. In later times, lime was used in agriculture and this area still has the remains of more modern kilns scattered throughout.

The third area, while still containing limestone and sandstone, also has much harder rocks, shaped during the Ice Age into such spectacular sights as the Whin Sill, a great ridge with a steep drop to the north. This was incorporated by the Romans into the defensive system. The Vallum, on the other hand, separates from the Wall and is built in the much easier ground at the bottom of the hill.

After Birdoswald (near Gilsland), there is a lot of soft red sandstone, not so good for building. Materials were hard to find and originally the turf wall was built here, before harder rocks were brought from elsewhere.

The final section of the Wall area, the salt marshes from Carlisle to Bowness, also presented difficulties in procuring materials. After the Romans left, it is no surprise that all of the stonework disappeared and was recycled in many of the buildings and villages along the way.

Just before the site of Milecastle 34, the Wall leaves the eighteenth century Military Road and turns up towards Sewingshields Crags. From here, for the next fourteen miles or so to Gilsland, the walker is away from the rush and noise of traffic, although not too far away from civilisation to frighten the amateur walker like myself. Being away from the road, there are now some spectacular remains. There were also more and more walkers and tourists, most of them friendly, even their dogs. A group of young German women stood outside the remains of Milecastle 35, shivering in the cold and I could understand just enough to realise that they were discussing King Arthur, the merits of last night's piss-up in Carlisle, and the rain which seemed to be falling much heavier now. I also passed an American family. Mum and Dad were in their late 40s and there were two kids, around sixteen years old. The male teenager was telling the rest of the clan that, 'Butter is made by butterflies, in the same way that wasps and bees make honey and marmalade.' I smiled in a superior sort of way and walked on.

The reference to King Arthur was, however, spot on, as you might expect from Germans. Around here there used to be a castle and there is a story that King Arthur, Queen Guinevere, and some of his Round Table were frozen and trapped inside the hall beneath the castle. They would remain stuck until someone should first blow a bugle, which had been left on a table near the entrance, and second, cut a garter with the 'sword of stone', which had also been left on the table. One day, the farmer at Sewingshields went exploring around the castle ruins. Amidst toads, lizards, bats and the frozen bodies of the king and others, he came across the table with the bugle, sword and garter. He cut the garter, but with the bodies now appearing to come to life, took flight and left before blowing the bugle. As he left, Arthur managed to shout out:

O woe betide that evil day,
On which this witless wight was born.
Who drew the sword – the garter cut,
But never blew the bugle-horn!

Thus Arthur remains trapped somewhere under the rocks on which I had been walking. Not quite the glorious end to his life as we are led to believe by Alfred, Lord Tennyson and the like, but just as credible. Arthur was a real person, a Briton who rebelled against the Anglo-Saxons in the sixth century, but his story and use by later politicians has been rewritten and embellished for their own purposes.

Another Arthurian story connected with Sewingshields surrounds the King's and Queen's Crags, half a mile to the north west and is quoted by Collingwood Bruce:

'King Arthur, seated on the farthest rock, was talking with his queen, who meanwhile, was engaged in arranging her "back hair". Some expression of the queen's having offended his majesty, he seized a rock which lay near him, and with an exertion of strength for which the Picts were proverbial, threw it at her, a distance of a quarter of a mile! The queen, with great dexterity, caught it upon her comb, and thus warded off the blow; the stone fell about midway between them, where it lies to this very day, with the marks of the comb upon it, to attest the truth of the story. The stone probably weighs about twenty tons!'

I hurried on past the growing crowds, with the rain gradually stopping, aiming for my lunchtime date at Housesteads. It was much harder going now and there is a certain depression which is caused by timing how long it takes to cover what seems to be a short distance. I reckoned I was now down to not much more than one mile per hour. I was also glad that there were no lunchtime pubs on the way today as, the combination of alcohol, slippery footing and heavy rucksack would have meant some sort of injury I'm certain.

I also noticed what are referred to as 'gaps' in the wall. One of these is 'Busy Gap', where during the turbulent times of the past, a way through the barrier was possible. In former Geordie times, a 'Busy Gap Rogue' was an unsavoury character. Another one is

'Milking Gap', east of Housesteads and presumably deriving its name from some sort of cow shelter.

Just before Housesteads, I came across the Knag Burn gateway, which was added to the wall in the fourth century to help with access to the fort. I could see Jo and Rufus, walking on the other side of the Wall, but found it impossible to make my way inside. English Heritage, who manage the site, force you to walk right past the fort, then turn back and down to the official entrance, which was more than a little annoying, though understandable.

As it was a bank holiday Monday, I was not surprised how busy the fort was, although generally it is the favourite of many who visit the Wall, despite the long uphill walk required from the car park just off the Military Road. Its original name was Vercovicium and again there is some dispute as to its meaning. Collingwood Bruce translates it as 'hilly place', others as 'the place of able fighters'. In size, it was about average – five acres – but its importance is probably emphasised by the extent of what still remains. Like the Wall here, its survival owes partly to its isolation. So far up the hill is the fort that there was no need to divert the

Vallum which is far below near the road. Like Chesters, it was connected with the Stangate.

At this stage of the walk, you are likely to go one of two ways. Either you get so used to the Wall and the rectangular playing card feel of the forts that you take the ancient ruins in your stride, or you get worryingly excited by the smallest deviation or unique detail. With my young impressionable son there, I played it cool and acted the former. Secretly there was one thing which was exciting me inside, and this was nothing more than the evidence of building alterations to the barrack blocks. I had also seen these at Chesters but without any feeling of excitement. Here at Housesteads, perhaps because there were no German cavalrymen, this detail fascinated me. In the fourth century one of the barrack blocks was rebuilt as a row of individual one or two roomed 'chalets'. It is unclear, like so many things, why this happened, but has been suggested that these were family units once the laws on marriage were relaxed, or perhaps just individual houses for members of the 'vicus' once Roman power eroded in Britain.

Far more spectacular are the remains of the granaries, great underground vaults where the Romans kept their grannies. Or perhaps it was grain. These were built on high, level ground in order to provide a secure and dry storage area for all sorts of foods. The raised ground also helped to some extent to keep vermin away from whatever was stored there. Vents in the walls helped with circulation.

The remains of the vicus here, just south of the fort on the downward slope, help to illustrate its size and extent. In 1801 Hutton counted twenty streets and estimated that the population would have been somewhere over two thousand. Buildings from the settlement eventually reached right up to the walls of the fort, though this was probably a later development. One of the buildings, when excavated, was found to hold two adult corpses buried under the floor. Under Roman law, burials had to take place outside any settlement, away from houses and public buildings. This, as well as the fact that one of the corpses had fragments of a knife in its ribs, seems pretty conclusive evidence that something untoward had happened here. Another example of early Northumbrian crime was the finding of a mould, used to make counterfeit coins.

After lunch, I walked back up to the Wall, still with both pairs of boots, plus some vaseline (a request which Jo had chosen tactfully not to question) and battled with the 'crowds', making for Steel Rigg, which was my aim for the day. I had booked into the youth hostel at Once Brewed and, after the luxury of Newbrough Park, was not looking forward to it too much.

I had a choice of following the Wall itself or the line of the Roman Military Way, just to the south. Inadvertently, I found myself on the Military Way, but chose to move up through some gorse to the Wall. The views here were spectacular, as they would be for the next day or so of walking, looking out over the cliffs. First I came across Milecastle 37, with the remains of an obvious arch at the gateway, and of the soldiers' rooms. The cliffs here are known as Cuddy's Crags, sometimes connected with St Cuthbert, but probably linked with horses (Scots). Then again, the Geordie word for fool is 'cuddy'. Who knows?

Cuthbert was the Bishop of Lindisfarne in the final two years of his life (he lived from 635-687AD). Lindisfarne, the Holy Island off the Northumbrian coast, became a centre of Christianity during the early period of Anglo-Saxon rule, before being destroyed by the Vikings in 793. Why this section of the Wall should be connected with the Bishop –

later Saint – was beyond me, and I prefer to think that it had something to do with Geordie idiots. Or Scottish horses. Or both.

From here I passed through a variety of Gaps – Rapishaw, Milking, Sycamore – and along various crags – Hotbank, Highshields, Peels – along a path which suddenly dropped and then just as quickly rose again. Sycamore Gap is spectacular in itself, a sheer drop on both sides, leading to a hollow, where lies a sprawling sycamore tree. It has become more famous since it was used in the opening sequence of the 1991 film *Robin Hood, Prince of Thieves*. It is clearly now one of the main photo opportunities along the Wall, and I managed to get mine, complete with Japanese tourists. Close by, and ignored by the crowds, I found the remains of two shielings. These were shelters used by shepherds in the summer months, when tending their animals. Temporary, yet permanent. They are the reason why so many of the sites near here use the word 'shiels' or 'shields'. Also nearby is a rock with the symbol of a swastika carved in it by the Romans.

The swastika has been used by many different peoples throughout history. It is over three thousand years old and swastikas have been found on pottery and coins dating from ancient Troy. The word is Sanskrit and derives from su (= 'good') and asti (= 'to be') and was used to represent life, sun, power, strength and good luck. Right up until its adoption – and subsequent widespread vilification – by the Nazis, it still had positive connotations. It was found on cigarette cases (before they themselves were deemed to be bad), postcards and coins. During the first world war (1914-1918) it was incorporated into the uniform of the American and Finnish military.

By the turn of the twentieth century, the symbol was already starting to be adopted by German nationalists – possibly because of its ancient Aryan origins. Some say that in its design there are four Ls – representing Luck, Light, Love and Life. This is clearly nonsense (the ancient cultures, from where the swastika originates, did not speak modern English), but it does emphasise its more peaceful meaning. For the Romans it was a sign of good luck, much like the phallus I had seen at Chesters.

Just after Milecastle 39, I arrived at Steel Rigg car park, and, turning south, made my way down the minor road to Once Brewed, to the youth hostel. The last time I had stayed in a hostel had been some fifteen years previously and things seemed to have changed. I remember we had to do some 'chores', such as wash up or sweep the room, but these days, due to health and safety requirements (according to the guy on the front desk), this was no longer allowed. Breakfast was also available, at extra cost, so staying here was essentially a slightly cheaper form of bed and breakfast. The hostel was full that night (for which they apologised) and therefore I was sharing a room with three other guys – a father and son from London, who were walking west to east – and someone else who I never got to meet. The Londoners were fine, although the father's feet looked horrendously sore, with burst blisters and bruising. They had been staying in hostels all the way, and therefore tomorrow were aiming for Acomb, south of Chollerford, which would be the longest day of their walk. With those feet? I had a lot of sympathy.

I had a shower and walked down to the pub at Twice Brewed, only a hundred metres away. There is also a visitors' centre here, which has a lot of leaflets, but is otherwise quite Spartan, and that's it. At the hostel, the lady on reception warned me that doors shut at 11pm, but the pub closed then, 'and there's nothing else to do here'. There are a few interesting versions of why there is a Once Brewed Hostel and Twice Brewed Pub. One is that General Wade visited here when building his road (i.e. clearly posthumously), and, visiting the inn, ordered some of the local beer. This was not to his taste and allegedly very weak, so he asked that it be brewed again. When he returned the next week, the 'twice-brewed' ale was much better and the name of the pub was changed in memory of the incident. When the youth hostel was built, in the 1930s, it was named 'Once Brewed' as here only teas would be served and one brewing would be enough.

Or so they say. William Hutton stayed at the original Twice Brewed pub in 1801 (now a house known as 'East Twice Brewed'), but only after some difficulty. At first the landlady tried to put him off by saying she did not know if there was any space.

'You must be so kind as to indulge me with a bed. I will be satisfied with any thing,' he pleaded.

She offered him a bed-share with a 'poor sick traveller'. When he refused, she then offered one with a ten year old boy, which he accepted. Later she eventually found him a whole bed of his own. He watched as fifteen 'carriers' were served a dinner of pudding ('about as big as a peck measure') and beef ('half a calf'). 'Every piece went down as if there was no barricade in the throat. One of those pieces was more than I have seen eaten at a meal by a moderate person. They convinced me that eating was the chief 'end of man'. The tankard too, like a lading bowl out of the well, was often emptied, often filled.'

I ordered a beer in the pub and tried to decide what to do next. There was what I took to be another pub, two hundred metres down the road, so after a while, I wandered down there, but it was only a hotel, selling expensive meals and I was quizzed by someone who came out as I peered in through the darkened glass.

I could of course have gone to Vindolanda, which is a mile away, but I had visited this site only a week or so earlier. Three generations of the Birley family have been involved in excavations here beginning in 1929 when Eric, an Oxford graduate and lecturer in archaeology at Durham University managed to buy a 240 acre farm at Bardon Mill for £4,000. This farm contained a house (an additional £400) and the remains of the Roman fort. In the early 1970s he set up the Vindolanda Trust, which now looks after the fort. When

Hunter Davies visited Eric and his wife in 1973, he was present when the couple received an abusive phone call – one of many. Apparently thirty years ago, there was an amount of hostility to the family and a belief that they were making money out of the fort (different days then). The hostility now seems to have disappeared, although the dynasty is still evident. Both of Eric's sons Anthony and Robin have been involved in excavating, as is his grandson, Andrew. Robin's wife, Pat, was also involved in the educational side of the trust. The trust also owns the Roman Army Museum and the site of the fort of Carvoran, both a little further to the east on the Stanegate.

Vindolanda differs from the other forts in two ways: firstly, it is now known by its original name, rather than the modern one (which is Chesterholm); secondly, it is not (despite the pleas from the otherwise faultless Vindolanda Trust) a Wall fort. It was built originally around 80 AD, as part of the Stanegate defences. At first there was a timber fort here, which had to be replaced every seven or eight years by another timber fort. At least five such forts were replaced in this way, before the first more permanent stone buildings were erected in the 140s.

As well as the remains of these forts, there is also substantial evidence of the civilian settlement, the vicus. Apart from a few bits and pieces at Housesteads, here are the only surviving remains of such a settlement, with taverns and houses, including a good example of a 'strip house'. The level of taxation charged in the settlement was based on the amount of frontage the owner's house held on the main street, so some were built so that this was as narrow as possible, thus giving the effect of a long and thin 'strip' of a house. There is also a later Christian church.

As each new fort was built on top of the older one, the depth of some of the remains here exceeds six metres (twenty feet). The anaerobic and marshy conditions ensured that a number of relics have survived to the present day including an incredible amount of footwear, as well as wooden objects and bronze or iron tools and equipment.

In the week in which Hunter Davies visited Vindolanda in 1973, during excavations of the vicus, two thin pieces of wood were found, stuck together. When separated, they were found to contain traces of what appeared to be handwriting. This find was rushed to an expert in Durham University for analysis, but by this time (only a few hours later), any such traces had disappeared. Fortunately infra-red photography was able to make out the remains of the script and after much work, the writing was deciphered as part of a letter to a soldier based at Vindolanda, promising the sending of a parcel containing shoes and underwear. This was the first of the Vindolanda Writing Tablets, of which nearly two thousand have since been discovered. 'Perhaps the wooden tablets will reveal all when they are analysed,' wrote Davies, still unaware of the huge significance of the find.

There are two types: Stylus tablets, usually made of wax-covered pine, accounting for twenty per cent of the tablets; and Leaf tablets, thin sheets of wood, specially prepared for ink writing. Two or three of these (1mm thick) tablets would be bound together: the message would go on the inner sheets and the address on the outside. These tablets (written in cursive script, without punctuation or dating) are a real mixture of military records, business transactions and private letters. All of them predate the Wall. One of the military reports from 90AD reveals that out of 750 men and six centurions at the fort, 450 men and five centurions were absent. Some were serving as a bodyguard for the provincial governor or procurator (finance officer), others had been sent to Corbridge. Of the 300 remaining, more than ten per cent were unfit for service, whether through injury or suffering from conjunctivitis.

Another military record has become famous for criticising the fighting skills of the natives, referring to them as 'Brittunculi', which is usually translated as 'the wretched Britons'. Inevitably this has been overplayed in recent years and has often been used to suggest that this one instance of name-calling meant that this was a universal Roman term of abuse for the British. History is not quite so simple.

Another famous letter is a party invitation from Claudia Severa:

'Claudia Severa to her Lepidina, greetings. I send you a warm invitation to come to us on September 11th for my birthday party, to make my day more enjoyable with your presence. Say "hello" to your Cerialis. My Aelius sends his best wishes to you and your sons.'

These tablets are the earliest written records from Britain and their importance for understanding life in the early years of Roman Britain, before the Wall, cannot be underestimated. There are some examples at the on-site museum, but most are held in London, at the British Museum, within special environmental conditions.

Also on site are remarkable replicas of sections of the Turf and Stone Walls, including parts of their respective timber and stone milecastles, and a ditch. These were built in 1973–4 by pupils of Heathfield High School in Gateshead. Interestingly (and giving us some indication of why the whole Wall was eventually made from stone), in the twenty years between 1972 and 1992, the Turf Wall replica lost over three feet of its height. Also notable is the fact that the students reckoned the most difficult part of their reconstruction was digging the ditch. Near to the fort is a Roman milestone, standing five feet high. This is the only Roman milestone in Britain still standing to its original height and in its original position.

I had seen this only a few days earlier, not expecting to have any time to make the detour during my week of walking, so was looking for something else to do. It was still only late afternoon, so I hit upon the idea of taking the Hadrian's Wall bus into Halt-whistle, some two and a half miles away for a look around.

Haltwhistle (meaning 'river junction

beside a hill') is a small town with a population of around 3,800 and claims to be 'The Centre of Britain'. This appears to be calculated by finding the mid-point of the longest north-south axis, from Orkney to Dorset. From here, in the centre of the town, distances to all other points of the compass end at an equal point where their opposite meets the sea (i.e. east and west, 26.5 miles to both Wallsend and Bowness; north-east and south-west, 50 miles to Alnmouth and Ravenglass). This is explained on a plaque in the town centre, but I must admit I got confused and sceptical. I had been to Wallsend and knew that there was land further east (South Shields with its Roman fort, Arbeia). And as for north and south, what about the Shetland Islands or Cornwall and Devon? I had a quick look around town, a terrible pint of Jennings in The Manor, and got the bus back to Twice Brewed.

In the pub I bumped into a headteacher from Carlisle and her husband (a headteacher from Haltwhistle – but I didn't quiz him about the fraudulent claims of the town). They had been completing the walk in stages over a few weeks and had just completed the stretch I would do tomorrow.

Looking out the window I saw a man and

two young boys (around nine or ten), walk by in the drizzle, with backpacks and sticks. Ten minutes later they arrived back in the pub. I overhead the guy ask if there were any rooms left at the pub (there were). They had originally planned to camp at the site just further down the road, but this was a lot further down the road than they had been led to believe. I toyed with the idea of booking in here too rather than the hostel, but having paid my money and struggled for half an hour with the 'hygienic' cotton sleeping bag, decided to make my way back to Once Brewed.

My room was in darkness (it was only just after 9.30pm), so I got undressed and into bed, taking ages to fall asleep. I was woken up by the snoring from two generations and visited the (now filthy) toilets. I made a mental note to look for a cheap hotel near Birdoswald the next day, rather than stay at the youth hostel there, as originally planned.

6

Once Brewed to Gilsland

Breakfast was still the 'Northumbrian' but disappointingly small and I was out and back on the trail by nine o'clock. First I had to face the long dull walk back up to the Wall, but once done, set off at a reasonably good pace and again with spectacular views to both north and south. I was soon slowed down by the sudden rising and dropping of the terrain, but was gradually getting higher and higher, reaching Winshields Crags, the highest point on the Wall, which the guide-books put at somewhere between 1,132 and 1,230 feet (around 350 metres).

Gradually more and more walkers appeared and at Cawfields Crags car park, I was overwhelmed by yet more young German women, one of whom had fallen on her arse into a cowpat. The traditional German characteristic of Schadenfreude (or taking pleasure in someone else's misfortune) was not openly shown I should report, although there were a few hidden sniggers from some of the bitchier girls in the group.

This part of the trail is also the Pennine Way and I met someone who was aiming for Slaggyford later that day. We both looked to the south, where the Pennines were hidden by menacing rain clouds. 'You should be alright,' he said, 'but I am going to get pissed on.' Five minutes later it started pouring down and I scrambled to get my waterproof coat on and the cover for my rucksack. As is inevitable with these things, by the time I had achieved this, soaking because I had apparently tried to put my waterproofs on inside-out, the rain had stopped. I took the coat off and the rain resumed.

The next fort I came to was Aesica or Great Chesters. The Roman name is thought to refer to a Celtic god called Esus. This is one of the smallest forts on the Wall and was built on the original site of Milecastle 43. I met up again with the walker doing the Pennine Way and followed him into the remains of the fort.

There is no doubt a certain psychology about our behaviour of that day. I had passed him just after Steel Rigg, once I had got to the top of the hill at the Wall, and had childishly somehow felt a trickle of glory flow through my veins as I took the lead. True, he had actually been stationery at that point, consulting his map, but somehow I was proving my virility by overtaking him. For the next mile or so I had felt him close behind me, but then he disappeared and a sudden loneliness came down on me. It did not help that I was then at the highest and most remote part of the Wall, and I kept looking over my shoulder with fading hope that I would ever see him again.

Then the cheating bastard overtook me. I was sitting down, having a drink of water when he sped past (no doubt only momentarily increasing his speed, for effect) with a patronising, 'Hello again'. As soon as there was a respectable distance between us, up I jumped, swung the rucksack on, and was after him, like a greyhound chasing a robotic hare. I was slowly gaining on him, when I noticed some menacing-looking cattle ahead, baying manically and running around in circles. I slowed down, willing to let my chum brave the possessed bovines before me, but then disastrously, and, in the middle of the frothy-mouthed Friesians, rather stupidly, he bent down to tie one of his bootlaces. The cows all, as one, turned their heads towards me, as if waiting to see what I would now do. I had no choice but to walk on, past the other guy, who looked up at me with an all-knowing smirk. For some reason I asked him if he needed, 'a hand with that.'

'What? My lace?' he said, pretending to be surprised, but actually, chivalrously, hiding his glee over the fact that he knew that I knew that he knew that I was scared of the cows. 'No, it's OK, it's snapped but I've got a spare one.' I hurried on, now determined to lose him and any memory of the episode with my speed. By the time I met the Germans at Cawfields, he was nowhere to be seen, but again, two minutes later while I sat drinking from my water bottle, he was standing next to me. I acted like I had never met him before, and it was only then that we had our first major exchange of conversation, where I found out that he was making for Slaggyford (I wonder whether he had decided to change his route simply to be kind to me?) and where he made his comment on the likelihood of rain.

By the time I reached Great Chesters, he was back in front, again a situation which I welcomed, as the remains of this fort and the route through it and out the other side are difficult to make out at first. Thus it happened that, as he inevitably made one error of judgement followed by another and he zig-zagged across the field, I followed him directly, walking three metres behind. Some-one came out of the farmhouse nearby and stood watching this charade in some amaze-ment.

Chesters fort, where I had seen the Roman cavalry display, is confusingly more famous and much bigger than Great Chesters. The name of both comes from the Latin 'castra', meaning 'army camp', a word which has filtered into many place names near the Wall and indeed throughout Britain (Rudchester, Haltonchesters, Cirencester, Chester, Cheshire, etc). Great Chesters is one of the smallest forts on the Wall, built after 128AD. There is evidence of an elaborate water supply, an aqueduct bringing water from a point some two and a quarter miles away to the north, but actually covering a distance of six miles, due to the nature of the ground.

As we moved back eventually towards the Wall ditch, my companion decided that it was time for me to go in front so he did the old 'tie-the shoelace' routine again and I overtook him. I passed by and never saw him again.

Walking towards Walltown Crags, I became aware that although just over halfway along the walk, I was about to leave the best of it behind. On the crags, there were quite a few people around: young Spaniards with heavy winter clothes, but still shivering under the overcast skies; middle-aged Japanese couples in their Sunday Best (or whatever the Japanese equivalent is), taking photos of anything that moved and anything that didn't; serious walkers with their waterproof maps and waterlogged shorts; German girls falling into cow shit (again); and so on. Near to here is King Arthur's Well another link with the legend. This is supposedly the spot where Edwin, King of Deira and then Northumbria (just before Oswald, mentioned previously), was baptised, following his conversion to Christianity in the year 626. 1 came down off the Wall and into the remains of the quarry at Walltown itself, heading for the Roman Army Museum, which is nearby and owned by those who also own part of Vindolanda.

In his 1992 book *Discovering Hadrian's Wall*, Dudley Green wrote about Walltown: 'It is hoped to develop the whole area as an historical and archaeological theme park based on the history of the Roman Wall and of Roman Britain in general.' Clearly (and possibly thankfully) this has not happened. Instead the area is currently being transformed into an area of wildlife and geological trails, under the auspices of the National Park.

At this point is the junction of the Stane-gate and the Maiden Way, a Roman road coming up from Kirkby Thore and over into modern day Scotland. A fort was built to guard this junction, probably originally dating back to long before the Wall and then rebuilt in the later years of Hadrian's reign. It is three and a half acres in size and its ancient name was Magnis or Magnae, apparently meaning the 'Stones', although I always thought that was the Latin word for 'big'. In its earlier years it was garrisoned by the first Cohort of Hamian (Syrian) Archers – the only known detachment of archers in Roman Britain. It is interesting that the bow and arrow as a weapon only rose to prominence in the Middle Ages. I wonder why this was the case? It seems a safe weapon to be unleashing at distance on your enemy. Perhaps it just wasn't required.

The vallum deviates to the north of the fort, rather than the south, which suggests that the fort was already there when the Wall was built. However a number of interesting Roman souvenirs have suggested that it was not thought of as part of the Wall, although very close to it. The Rudge Cup, found in

Wiltshire in 1725, is a small enamelled cup which once formed part of a set of ornamental souvenir bowls. This cup is decorated with pictures of the Wall, forts, milecastles and also the names of four of the forts on the wall: Mais (Bowness), Aballava (Burgh), Uxellodunum (Stanwix), Camboglanna (Castlesteads) and Banna (Birdoswald). A similar bowl was found in Amiens in 1949 containing also the name of Aesica.

In 2003 a further bowl was found, this time in Staffordshire, which contains the names of Mais, Coggabata (Drumburgh), Uxelodunum and Cammoglanna. The inclusion of the very small fort at Drumburgh is very useful to historians as the spelling differs by more than the usual margin of error. The previously accepted name was Concavata or Congavata. It is also interesting, and in some ways comforting, that the Romans themselves saw the Wall as a useful opportunity for souvenir exploitation.

I made for the Roman Army Museum, just a few hundred metres down towards the Military Road, in search of some lunch (the meagre youth hostel breakfast long since used up). I didn't want to actually visit the museum itself as I have been on a few occasions at other times, but I was allowed to buy a sandwich, look at the souvenirs available for purchase, obviously, and sit in the café, as long as I did not want to use the toilet. I am sure this contravenes some sort of health and safety/planning regulations, but I was OK. Having turned into some feral, unshaven beast during the previous few days, I had learned how to 'go' outdoors, a habit which I had so far avoided in my adult life (except for one unfortunate drunken incident as a student in Edinburgh; well how was I to know there was someone asleep under the pile of newspapers?).

There were two kinds of troops in the Roman Army. The first were the legions. Each legion consisted (by the time of the early empire) of around five thousand men, all of whom were Roman citizens. A legion was commanded by a 'legate' of senatorial rank, who had been commissioned by the Emperor. Next in the power line came the senior tribune, followed by the Prefect of the Camp, then five equestrian Tribunes. The equestrian order (or 'knights') was at first a wealth distinction, originally created to form the army's cavalry, but later became a social distinction.

The legion was split into sixty centuries. As you might expect each century had once consisted of a hundred men, but by now that number had decreased to around eighty. In charge of each century was a Centurion. The century was then split into ten contubernia, a group of eight which usually billeted together. Each legion also had a unit of cavalry, numbering around one hundred and twenty.

Thus:

1 contubernium was 8 soldiers;

10 contubernia = 80 soldiers = 1 century;

60 centuries = 4,800 soldiers = 1 legion

The second type of troops were the Auxiliaries, who were not automatically Roman citizens. Unlike the legionaries, they did not have heavy armour and many used their traditional and local weapons. The Auxiliary Troop was a much smaller unit than the Legion, being either a 'quingenary' cohort of 480-500, or a 'milliary' cohort of just under one thousand. It could consist either of infantry (again split into centuries) or part-cavalry, where the cavalry contingent was known as an 'ala' and split into 'turmae' of around thirty to forty men, with each turma led by a Decurion.

Unlike the legionaries, the auxiliaries were not Roman citizens, although they would have been presented with the gift of citizenship once they had completed their twenty five years of service. The auxiliaries also had the misfortune of taking the first brunt of any fighting, usually in the hope that the legions, following behind, would not be required. As regards the Wall, the three Legions stationed in Britain built it – there is no evidence of local slave labour being used, as is sometimes thought – and then they left it to be manned by the Auxiliaries.

As the Roman army had been raised from its many provinces, this has given rise to speculation and sympathy for poor Mediterraneans, Africans, and so on, shivering as Auxiliaries stationed in the bleak terrain and climate of Northumbria and Cumbria. This has some truth in it and we can see this from the names of the cohorts stationed there. At Segedunum there was first a Cohort of the Nervians, then one of Lingones, both from what is now France. At Aesica were the II Asturum Equitata, originally raised in north west Spain. At Onnum, the Ala I Pannoniorum Sabiniana (Hungary); at Carvoran, the I Hamiorum Sagittariorum (Syria), and so on. Only at Pons Aelius (Newcastle) was there some 'British' connection: the I Cornoviorum were stationed there, originally raised from the area of modern Shropshire. However, although these units would have originated in far-away places, replacements would have been raised locally, so after a couple of generations, the name of the cohort would have borne little resemblance to its racial mix.

I finished my coronation chicken sandwich and negotiated my way through the tightly packed café. The tables were very close together although the place itself was actually quite empty. One other group was there, a family cohort from London, politely discussing driving to York as the weather would no doubt be better there. Outside it was raining quite heavily now, so I put my waterproofs on and headed in the direction of Gilsland.

I passed Thirlwall Castle, the ruins of an impressive stronghold built by John Thirlwall around 1330. The surname means something like 'gap in the wall' – no doubt a local place which the family adopted, and which has appropriately transferred to the 'castle', built, as was so often the case, mainly out of Roman-cut stone. Again here is evidence of trouble in the borders – this time the Border Reivers.

For around four hundred years, between the thirteenth and sixteenth centuries, this area of the country was held to ransom by the exploits of armed bands of raiders, split into family groups, who would come and steal your livestock, burn your property, and probably kill you if they got the chance. It wasn't a case of English against Scots, more a case of every man for himself, united with his clan or family in search of plunder.

The Reivers, as they became known, from the verb reive meaning 'to steal' (and giving us the word 'bereaved'), were not confined to any one class, and those from the upper classes defended themselves from each other by building fortress-houses known as peles. These were usually three or four storeys high: the ground floor sheltered the animals and the living quarters would be higher up. There would also be a bell or a beacon in the roof, to raise the alarm. Interior furnishings were minimalist, unsurprisingly under the circumstances. The lower class version of this was the bastle, a similar construction, but with walls not quite so thick.

In 1248, a Border Law (Legs Marchiarum) was agreed between six English and six Scottish knights. This included provisions for the return of fugitives to their country for the recovery of debts and the trial of accused persons (for crimes ranging from murder to arson) at a set time and place. The area on both sides of the border was split into units known as Marches: there were three of these on each side – West, Middle and East. Each March had its own Warden, who reported to the king of the relevant country, but who seemed to have ruled with a fair degree of autonomy. Their duties were originally to administer the Border Laws, but this extended to all matters related to keeping the peace within their area. They were expected to co-operate with their colleagues over the border, but, perhaps inevitably, this did not always work out quite so well. Incidentally an English Warden was paid anywhere between £300 and £1,100 per annum, while his poor Scottish counterpart received around £20.

Despite the efforts of the Wardens, often the only hope the ordinary Borderer had was to pay protection money to one or other of the Reiving families. This was called 'black rent' or 'black mail', which gives us another word still used today. One area of the Borders was notoriously and literally lawless. The 'Debateable Land' was a narrow strip of four miles by twelve miles between the Rivers Esk and Sark. Neither country took ownership of this with the resulting devastation over the centuries. A commission finally settled the issue in 1551 by building a wall (where did they get that idea from?), known as the Scots dyke. Traces can still be seen today.

In this atmosphere then it is not surprising to find buildings like Thirlwall in the area. After the Union of the Crowns in 1603, peace gradually took hold in the borders and many of the peles and bastles fell into disrepair, although some are still used today, often as farm houses. Thirlwall was sold to the Earl of Carlisle in 1748 for £4,000, but largely ignored after that time.

After turning round on myself and crossing a stream, I found myself back on the B6318, the Military Road built after 1745, which I had left a couple of miles before Housesteads. This lasted only for a few minutes before turning left into a field. There were suddenly four or five groups of walkers, all heading in the same direction as myself. I passed a couple of guys who were talking about trying to find a place to stay that night either in Gilsland or Brampton and began to panic that everyone had the same idea and I would have to resign myself to another night in a youth hostel. I accelerated past one group, then the next, not even slowing down when I came across an obviously mad calf which was jumping about all over the place, while its mother kept a careful eye on me.

Leading the race towards Gilsland I then found myself in someone's back garden, watched by a throng of garden gnomes. I was seriously worried that I had lost my way amid my haste, particularly when I heard the manic barking of three or four dogs. The noise didn't seem to be getting any closer however and I finally found a trail path arrow pointing the way. Then came the long but slight descent into Gilsland, watching over my shoulder in case my rivals were about to run past me and book the last room available. I worked out a detailed plan whereby I would pretend to hurt my ankle and beg them to carry me to Gilsland where I would clearly be offered the room. Such was my level of paranoia and insanity by this stage.

Gilsland lies exactly on the county border between Northumbria and Cumbria, near the site of Milecastle 48. In Victorian times this was a spa resort, but no longer. In Roman times, the River Irthing, which runs near the town, marked the boundary between the original stone and turf walls, and then, when all was stone, between the narrow wall on broad foundations running east, and the narrow wall on narrow foundations, to the west.

I made for the Station Hotel and sat inside (it had begun to rain again) with a bottle of beer. There were rooms available here, but for some reason I decided not to ask for one straightaway – bizarre and calm, considering my panic of a few moments earlier. The pub soon filled up with the walkers I had recently overtaken, but I noticed that none seemed eager to opt for a room here either. The hotel looked pleasant enough, if anything a little quiet, run by a Scottish couple and what I took to be their three teenage sons, one of whom had a Scottish accent, the younger ones a more local one. I had decided to look around the village a bit, perhaps even for the legendary Romanway guest house where Hunter Davies had stayed in 1973 and which had been fully booked when Harrison had attempted to get a room in 1954.

Having finished my beer I wandered outside and onto the main road through Gilsland, looking out for the Romanway. In 1973 the guest house had been owned by a Ron Dawkins who kept hundreds of budgies and finches in the cellar. In the garden was one of the best preserved sections of the Wall, plus two altars, which guests used to clean their boots. Passing the post office and village shop I realised I had left my stick at the pub, so returned there, taking the chance to have another beer and shelter from the much heavier rain. Back out on the main street again, walking towards the school where the Wall appeared again on the other side of the road, I came across a derelict house whose gardens looked a bit like a scrap yard: cars and old horse boxes with trees growing in them, chickens running around. I looked at the house with its decomposing walls and half-roof and saw the sign on the side: 'Romanway'. Having seen no other potential place offering accommodation, I decided just to continue on to Birdoswald and book in at the hostel. I could always return to Gilsland later that day for something to eat, so I hurried, alongside the Wall to Willowford Farm and Bridge and beyond to Birdoswald.

Two minutes later, the rain restarted, much heavier than before, so I rang directory enquiries from my mobile, was put through to the Station Hotel and booked a room. If the owners were surprised to see me enter their pub for the third time within an hour, they kept it hidden. I was shown to my room, which was clean, warm (and private), had a shower, got changed and wandered outside to go and check on the remains of the milecastle which I had so far failed to look at.

Milecastle 48 is known as the Poltross Burn Milecastle and, along with 37 near Housesteads, is one of the better-preserved fortlets. Considering that the Carlisle-Newcastle railway runs only feet away across the top of the Wall, its survival is even more remarkable. Each milecastle was between 250 and 300 square metres and contained sleeping quarters for anywhere between twelve and thirty soldiers. At Poltross Burn there are remains of a flight of stairs, suggesting that the rampart walkway here was fifteen feet (4.6m) above ground level.

I then made a guilty phone call to the Birdoswald Youth Hostel, cancelling my booking to an answerphone. Its inability to reply or argue with me or tell me that I would be charged a fee for the late cancellation (which I had expected), unfortunately led me on in my awkwardness to mention something about abandoning my walk and the illness of my baby son and possibly also some leg injury added in to the bargain. Shameful.

Back in the village I made for the post office where I would hopefully be pointed in the direction of a cash machine (I had less than £4 on me), or failing that, where I would be able to cash a cheque, although I would probably have to pay a fee. Of course, there was no cash machine in the village, as the couple who worked in the place told me with some degree of glee. Would they cash a cheque then? Ah, depends which bank you're in. Which banks were OK? Which bank was I in? Royal Bank of Scotland. Sorry not allowed. Possibly a local by-law dating back to the time of the Reivers.

I left the post office, trying to work out my options. Perhaps the hotel would let me pay by card or cheque. Perhaps they would cash a cheque. But I would have the same problem tomorrow night at Walton, a village which was even smaller than Gilsland. I must have been talking to myself, because I was suddenly addressed by a lady standing at the bus stop which I had now reached. 'There's a bus to Brampton in two minutes.' I looked at the timetable stuck to the pole and sure enough, my few coins would be enough to take me into Brampton, where I would have an hour to kill before catching the return back to Gisland. I knew Brampton – there were definitely cash machines there. There seemed no real choice to make and ten minutes later I found myself being dropped off in the centre of the small market town.

It was an eerie and uncomfortable feeling just being there. I was only three miles from the village where I lived – the bus I got was the one I caught most days when travelling into Carlisle – and felt again the sadness of knowing that I was coming close to the end of my experience, as well as some hedonistic guilt of being so close to home, but about to travel further away again and spend some money in a hotel. I defended this to myself by arguing that a stop at home would some-how tarnish the whole experience – and what also helped was I knew there would be no-one there; my wife and son were still in the north east, having continued there after stopping for lunch with me at Housesteads.

Still I sat, almost hiding in the White Lion, reading the *Cumberland News*, hoping no-one would recognise me. Brampton is a nice little market town, nine miles to the east of Carlisle, with good schools, good takeaways, a bored and displaced teenage population, a lot of pubs, some shops, a doctor's surgery and a statue of Hadrian, marking Cumbria's claim to the Wall country. There is also a cash-point.

The town dates back to Roman times, but its name is derived from The Old English for 'brambles' or perhaps 'broom'. In 1252, King Henry granted the town a Market Charter, thus enabling that omnipresent title of 'market town', which it shares with so many others. In 1745, Bonnie Prince Charlie stayed here, en route to London. Coincidentally, in the Howard Arms pub (still there), six of Charlie's men were sentenced to death a year later. They were hanged from a large tree in the town, the Capon Tree, so-called because those unfortunate enough to be executed there had their caps nailed on the tree. Allegedly.

Another story is that, as well as being the open-air death chamber for criminals, it was also the spot where the local judges would sit and eat their lunch in the afternoon sunshine, no doubt happily discussing whose lives they were about to terminate. Their lunch may, from time to time, just possible, perhaps, have included ... capon chickens. Yes. Perhaps an even more tenuous link.

A much more interesting and certainly more credible story comes from the nearby village of Croglin. Here, just after the English Civil War (1642-6), the owners of Croglin Low Hall, the Fishers, decided to move from the area, and they rented out the hall to two brothers and sisters from the Cranswell family. During the hot summer, the sibling tenants slept with their windows open. One hot sticky night, the sister lay naked in her bed, covers cast aside, window closed, but shutters unfastened.

Unable to sleep she looked out of the window into the half-light of a Cumbrian midsummer night, and saw what appeared to be two lights in the trees some distance away, towards the nearby graveyard. Mesmerised she began to make out a dark shape which was moving towards her window. Suddenly afraid, she froze in panic, unable to do anything until the shape disappeared from view, perhaps 'flying' above or around the side of the house. She jumped up and ran towards her bedroom door – which she had locked earlier. As she struggled with the key she became aware of the shape again, now at the window, and apparently trying to dislodge the glass from the window pane.

It succeeded and then it was on her, its fingers in her hair, its teeth sinking into her throat. She screamed, and her brothers came running, battering down the door to rescue her. The creature fled through the window.

After that, the young woman always kept her shutters closed at night and the brothers carried pistols around the house, all believing they had been attacked by some local lunatic. Inevitably, one night the sister heard a scraping at her window. She lifted her candle and walked towards it, where she saw the shrivelled decaying face and bony hands of the creature which had attacked her before. Immediately she screamed and her brothers came rushing in. The 'vampire' escaped again, although not before being hit in the leg by a well-aimed gunshot.

After this incident the Cranswells, the tenants of Croglin Low Hall, met with their neighbours, the tenants of Croglin High Hall and discovered that they had suffered the same terror. The young daughter there had also been bitten in the neck. They made their way to the nearby graveyard and entered one of the vaults. Within the vault, the mangled remains of corpses and coffins lay all around in a violent mess. One coffin had been left untouched. Lifting its lid they came across the ghastly figure which had appeared at the window of Croglin Low Hall the previous night. Looking at the shrivelled leg, they saw a fresh gun wound.

Action was taken immediately and the coffin and the Croglin Vampire were burnt on the spot.

As with most horror stories, this is not the end of the tale.

In the early twentieth century, a fire broke out in the dining room chimney of Croglin

Low Hall. When it was out the then tenant found an ancient burnt corpse within the chimney. The tenant decided, whoever it was, was due a decent Christian burial, but mysteriously, he died before being able to do this. Perhaps the corpse is still there...

I was relieved when the bus back to Gilsland picked me up just after six o'clock, particularly when I realised that there was no-one on it whom I recognised. By this stage of the journey (it was going on to Hexham), there was only one other passenger – a woman of about my age who was drinking a can of Special Brew, but who otherwise looked pleasant enough. She even nodded and said hello, almost in a flirtatious manner as I sat across from her, offering her can to me. The whole experience in Brampton had made me very uncomfortable and nervous, but I had enough courage to decline.

As we approached Gilsland, I noticed that we sped past a sign saying 'Road Ahead Closed', but was reassured by the driver's confidence in ignoring it. We certainly hadn't encountered any problems in the other direction, but then I had not been paying too close attention to the journey and may have come on one of the other roads. Sure enough after a mile or so, we came to a halt: the road ahead was closed and the driver came up to me, at first to hit me I thought, but simply to ask my advice. I pleaded ignorance. 'Sorry mate, I don't come from round here,' I explained in what I hoped was a southern/London sort of accent, which unfortunately came out half Welsh, half Pakistani, much to the obvious suspicion of the driver and the girl with the Special Brew.

The driver got out, had a word with some members of a small crowd who had now gathered around us, came back in the bus and spent the next thirty minutes slowly reversing and swearing and casting evil glances in my direction. As we passed by each farmhouse on the route, its occupants suddenly appeared, as if waving us on. Dogs barked and children cheered the huge reversing vehicle (it was, of course, mostly uphill). Finally we came to a place where the driver was able to reverse in and turn the bus around and so continue the journey normally. There was a sense of relief from all three of us and for her part my fellow passenger emitted a loud and fragrant belch, before staring at me with her come-and-get-me eyes and opening another can of beer, which sprayed all over her face and jacket.

'You couldn't make it up,' she said, smiling. No, I replied, you certainly couldn't.

Back at the Station Hotel, I went down to the bar and ordered some food. Mindful of my cash situation I paid for both the room and the meal with a card, and sat down to wait, reading some more of the papers I had bought in Brampton and watching a local snooker tournament which was taking place in the bar. I also noticed the man and two young boys whom I had seen at Twice Brewed the night before. They were all arguing over who should get to choose the music on the juke box.

After an hour I asked, in that nervous, don't want-to-cause-any-trouble, British sort of way, how long the food would be as I was starving and the landlady suddenly realised she had completely forgotten about my order. I staved off my hunger with a complimentary bag of peanuts, and when the food (Cumberland Sausage – although I was still just in Northumberland) finally did appear, it was delicious. The staff (i.e. the multi-accented family) were very apologetic throughout the rest of my stay there, obviously blaming mum's/the wife's forgetfulness – but there was no need to be. I had felt rather guilty about a lot of the day's activities – cancelling the youth hostel booking, being in Brampton, pissing against the Wall of the Roman Army Museum when they wouldn't let me use the toilet – no, I made that last one up – and I didn't want anyone else to feel any more guilt.

After tea I retired to bed. Closing the curtains in my room, I noticed a couple of tents pitched outside in the pub garden: perhaps the father and two sons who had been in the pub? This was confirmed next morning as I sat eating a wonderful breakfast and saw one of the boys pass by, his incongruous rucksack weighing him down and a small thick branch in his hand, a makeshift walking stick.

7

Gilsland to Walton

The rain and grey clouds of the previous two days had now disappeared and the sun was peering out from behind some fluffy cotton wool scuffs across the sky as I set out on the Wednesday, the sixth day of the trip.

This would be the shortest day of walking, but there would be quite a lot to see, including, sadly, the last few remaining bits of Wall still standing.

I was also saying farewell to Northumberland, the modern descendant of the great Anglo-Saxon kingdom which came together after the Romans had left and which had briefly been the most powerful area in England. I passed the ruins of the Romanway Guest House again, crossed the road and followed the Wall down towards Willowford Farm and the River Irthing. The Romans had built a bridge here, the remains of which can still be seen and where, as at Chesters, the abutment now stands a few metres away from the riverbank. Until recently passing this way meant paying a fee at the farmhouse and then returning to cross the river via the Military Road, or wading across the shallow river. In 1920, Jessie Mothersole noticed a little girl sitting in a wooden chair which was suspended from a wire, tied to the trees at each side of the bank. The little girl then pulled herself across the river using this contraption. Jessie, having politely asked permission from the nearby farm, then proceeded to use it many times. No-one at the farm knew what to call this invention, though at Birdoswald she was told that it was 'a sort of aeroplane'. Thankfully this aeroplane has long since disappeared and to mark the opening of the trail, a new award-winning footbridge has been built, and I crossed over this, ascended the steep bank at the other side and found myself among the remains of Milecastle 49 (Harrow's Scar), built over an original Turf Wall milecastle and later itself built over, by a post-medieval cottage.

For the next third of a mile, there is a very good stretch of surviving Wall. There are also a number of centurial stones – stones inscribed with the details of the soldiers who had built that particular stretch – but they are very hard to see, and although I walked up and down that bit for half an hour or so, I gave up in the end and walked towards Birdoswald Fort.

After years of debate, it seems finally accepted that the Roman name for this fort was Banna, which probably means 'promontory'. Although the remains are not as 'in your face' as at Chesters and Housesteads, Birdoswald is set in a spectacular location, overlooking the Irthing Gorge and with views south and west towards the Lake District fells and north, far into Scotland.

When I arrived at the entrance, the doors were still locked and there waiting for their Hadrian's Wall passports to be stamped were the family group who had been camping outside the Station Hotel in Gilsland. We soon got chatting – they were Keith, the father, and his two sons, Connor and Danny, who were nine and ten years old. I told them how remarkable and brave it was for the kids especially to walk such a long way, particularly when they were mainly camping, with only a couple of nights in bed and breakfasts. That first time I had seen them, as they walked past and then returned to the pub at Twice Brewed, they had been aiming for the campsite down the road, but had given up when they realised how far it was from any shops or pubs. Last night they had slept outside the hotel, where I was warm and dry. Tonight they were aiming for a bed and breakfast close to Irthington, then one more night of camping west of Carlisle, before finishing on the same day as me. They were pushing on and not visiting the fort, so I wished them well, and agreed to try and meet up with them in the Kings Arms at Bowness at the end of the walk, two days later.

As I had quite a lot of time that day, I decided to have a leisurely look around

Birdoswald, keeping well away from the youth hostel. I felt like I had a huge arrow pointing towards me, explaining who I was and what I had done the night before.

The views from the back (south) of the fort over the gorge are spectacular. From the front, i.e. the Military Road, apart from the Wall running east back towards Harrow's Scar (which was only uncovered in the 1930s), Birdoswald looks nothing like a Roman fort. When Hunter Davies came here in the early 1970s, he wrote: 'The fort gates at Birdoswald are some of the best to be seen anywhere, despite being in constant use today as the farm gates, with cars and tractors going through them all the time.' With this in mind, it is interesting to trace the history of the place over the past 2,000 years – giving us a picture not just of this area of North Cumbria, but indeed of what happened in England after the Romans left.

Before the fort was built, the area was one of dense woodland, probably with a peaty marsh in the middle. This was drained and the trees cleared away, and the Turf Wall was built, including the original stone turret (49a). The fort was then built, with the Turf Wall running up to its middle, thus leaving the fort projecting north of the Wall. The

Stone Wall was built further north, along the edge of the fort, finally encompassing it.

Originally the substantial fort would have held around one thousand soldiers, but by the early 400s, this number had dwindled to around one hundred. These troops would, of course, now have been well and truly of northern British descent, whatever the name of their unit. We have already seen that what we mean by the Romans leaving Britain did not mean a mass exodus of soldiers, evacuating to a land they had never seen. Probably it is more accurate to talk of Britain falling out of Roman administration. The soldiers would have stayed and their first problem would be that their pay would have stopped. Evidence however does not suggest that the soldiers then gave up and melted back into the civilian population. Perhaps they managed to 'persuade' the local people to pay some sort of protection or insurance money and the garrison stayed there for some time – possibly still calling themselves Roman and believing that that brought a certain legitimacy to their continued existence. All this is conjecture: we will never really know, but it is highly likely that during the first few centuries of the post-Roman period, Birdoswald continued as a Romano-British settlement.

The evidence goes quiet, through the appropriately named 'dark ages', until the thirteenth century when records show the fort, as part of the Barony of Gilsland, being looked after by a certain Walter Bevin. The fort passed through various hands, and to deal with the Scottish wars and the Reivers, a fortified house was built on the site sometime between the twelfth and fifteenth centuries.

In 1599, a schoolmaster from Appleby, Reginald Bainbrigg visited the site and wrote: 'Frome Lanercost I followed the Wall all ruinated, til I came to Birdoswald, whiche doth seame to have bene some great towne by the great ruynes thereof. The inhabitants did shew me the plaice where the church stode, the inscriptins ther are either worn out by the tracte of tyme or by the clownishe and rude inhabitants defaced.'

As well as the reference to Lanercost, a mile away from the Wall with its Priory built almost entirely from Roman Wall stones, the reference to the church shows at least some degree of development on the site. I wonder who the 'clownishe and rude inhabitants' were?

In a survey of 1603 a stone house is noted at Birdoswald, belonging to Thomas

Tweddle. A relative, Henry Tweddle, had possession of a cottage which had been built within the Harrow Scar milecastle, the remains of which I had seen earlier.

The house which is still standing was built from 1745, by the Bowman family. In 1802, Hutton had visited William Bowman where he was, 'received with that coldness which indicates an unwelcome guest, bordering upon a dismission'. However, his tenacity (which he compared with an expert angler playing with his fish before he catches it) and politeness led them to become, 'exceedingly friendly; so that the family were not only unwilling to let me go, but obliged me to promise a visit on my return.'

In the 1830s, excavations of the fort began and a decade later, having been purchased by Henry Norman, the mock medieval pele tower (still standing) was built.

In 1984, Birdoswald passed to the Treasury, in lieu of death duties for the landowner Lord Henley. In fact it came into the hands of Cumbria County Council. The excellent stewardship since then (along with donations from private firms, principally British Nuclear Fuels) has led to recent excavations, development and the present visitor centre, opened in 1993. At the time of writing, the county council is discussing the possibility of disposing of this asset, hopefully to a body like English Heritage which will continue the good work undertaken over the past twenty years.

So there you have a sketched history of one of the forts on the Wall. As regards its name, it is a mixture of an Anglo-Saxon name (Oswald – but unlikely to be the victor of Heavenfield, whose wooden cross I had seen earlier in the week) and the Celtic 'buarth', meaning, unsurprisingly, 'fort', (uncannily like the Anglo-Saxon 'burgh').

Of the Roman remains themselves, the most impressive aspects are the east gate and the granaries, built between 205 and 208 by Aurelius Julianus, commander of the Dacians (originally raised in what is now Romania). This information comes from an inscription found there. Two other inscriptions, both tombstones, give a more poignant reminder of life in those times. One, which was later re-used as a paving stone, refers to the death of the same commander's son, an infant called Aurelius Concordius who died aged one year and five days old. The other was set up by the brother of Decuibalus and Blaesus, the latter who died aged ten.

I had a cup of coffee in the café there,

which was now starting to fill up with hikers talking a mixture of different languages. One couple appeared to be Dutch, while an extended family talked hurriedly to each other in Spanish. After my coffee, I rejoined the trail, keeping an eye out for the remains of the Turf Wall, which can be seen just to the south of the road. The road is, once again, built pretty much on top of the Wall and the northern ditch and southern Vallum can clearly be made out.

I have incorporated a number of references to other books in this chapter, but finally I think it is worth pointing out an extract from the ever-observant and sarcastic Harrison commenting as he walked along the Military Road:

'I met practically no traffic here, save a large American car covered with baggage and carrying a man and woman sitting at opposite ends of the wide front seat, as if they were contemplating mutual separation. Another such had decanted a party while I was at Birdoswald, to whom I tried to explain the lay-out of the fort.' Unfortunately the Yanks seemed rather disinterested, and kept asking Harrison if he had seen the wall at London-derry, causing him to remark, possibly biting his tongue, that, 'no doubt the wind made antiquarian curiosity rather difficult.'

I soon came to Pike's Hill Signal Tower, a Roman observation post built before the Wall and then incorporated into it. This was an ideal position for watching over the Stanegate and a fort some way to the south at Nether Denton. The views to the south are pretty impressive and a sign points out the tops of the mountains as far away as Scafell Pike.

As I entered the remains of the Signal Tower, I noticed a sign indicating that there was a bull in the field I had just been in. Fortunately I had seen neither the bull, nor the sign at the other side, otherwise I would be having the same debate that a couple of other walkers, going in the opposite direction, were now having. I tried to reassure them that I had seen no animal in there and after the girl had lectured us all on the callousness of the farmers who were trying to kill anyone who dared to use the 'public, yes, PUBLIC' footpaths and who trod on their land, they eventually continued on their way. I sat down in the shade of the stonework (the sun was blazing again) and had some lunch, some rolls and cold meat I had bought the previous day in Brampton.

South of the Wall here, at Coombe Crag, is an old Roman quarry, where we have the inevitable inscriptions, naming a Securus, a Maternus and a Iustus, as well as an unhappy fellow calling himself Daminius. 'I did not want to do it,' he wrote, presumably referring to the quarrying, or otherwise showing his displeasure at the enforced graffiti writing he was made to carry out by his three so-called mates. Also here is a forged date of 210AD, actually giving the names of the Consuls (two senior offices of state, a device used then to denote the year), Faustinus and Rufus. The interesting thing here is that perhaps someone, at a much later date, was trying to give weight to the now discredited theory that the Wall had been built during Severus' reign, rather than under Hadrian, a hundred years earlier. On the other hand it is quite possible that additional building (and quarrying) did take place in 210 – but the carved names are much later than this. This is a strange type of vandalism and archae-ological fraud – carried out by boffins.

The village of Banks consists of nothing more than a few houses, but I was looking for one in particular. In the early 1970s when Hunter Davies was doing his walk, he came across a white farmhouse on the left-hand side of the road, with a notice on it saying 'LYC Museum. Welcome Friends.' LYC was

Li Yuan-Chi, who had opened this museum in the middle of nowhere, coming from China, via Italy and London. He seemed eccentric to say the least, an artist who had opened his own studio here, but had turned the place into an exhibition of other works, plus some reproduction souvenirs of the Roman Wall. Unsurprisingly he complained to Davis of getting lonely, 'I would like someone to discuss my museum with.'

Sadly, like the Romanway in Gilsland, the LYC Museum was no longer open.

Having passed through Banks, I turned off to the right, heading now for Walton. I met the last remaining piece of Wall at Hare Hill. Until recently, this short stretch, standing three metres high, was thought to be the highest surviving remnant of the Wall. However, like much elsewhere, this has been substantially rebuilt (in the nineteenth century), albeit using the original stones. One of these has an inscription 'PP', showing that it was built by a century of men under a 'Primus Pilus', or chief centurion within a legion.

From here to Walton, walking through farmland, there is some evidence of the ditch and raised land shows where the Wall had been. A dog came running towards me, barking loudly.

One of the biggest issues for me while doing the walk was my fear of the unpredictable behaviour of animals. As a child I have been bitten on the bum by dogs, watched our pet dog go for the throat of my brother, been knocked to the ground by a mad cow and chased across a dual carriageway by an unusually amorous sheep. As a young adult, working during my university vacation as a postie on the outskirts of Edinburgh, I have been attacked by all sorts of animals, from poodles to parrots, and once by a large rabbit. Its owner had waited until I had broken the news that her giro hadn't come in the post before setting Bugs Bunny on me.

So far on this walk I had come across relatively few animals and having prepared myself for at least three minor attacks and the probable loss of a finger, felt that something was building up. The first dog, in the train carriage at Newcastle, had been (too?) friendly. The cow, standing in my path, just after Rudchester, had simply been attracted by my singing. At Newbrough, the dog was noisy, but too old (and pissed, in my opinion). The Friesian cattle after Once Brewed were simply inquisitive, and more interested in the mental and physical battle between the Pennine Way walker and I, than in charging at us till we shat ourselves. Even the mad calf near Gilsland was probably just enjoying the exuberance of having being born in the first place. Finally the bull at Banks had been non-existent.

Other writers had commented on the animals they had met on the trip. The worst experiences seem to have happened to Jessie Mothersole who was chased by 'two huge specimens of the pig tribe.' Having escaped, she can hardly have been reassured by the explanation given at a local farmhouse, that the chase had been the result of the pigs' hunger.

Elsewhere, approaching Carlisle, as I have said earlier, she was attacked by a pack of greyhounds who grabbed her lunch from her pockets and ran off with it.

I felt for her. You will have picked up by now that dogs are one of my least favourite animals – they smell, are loud, have sharp teeth, are insane and, unlike cats, far too mad and energetic for their own good. This one showed no signs of fatigue as it raced a full quarter of a mile towards me. 'This is it,' I thought, 'having seen all of the Wall there is to see, I am going to have my throat torn out by this rabid, blood thirsty canine.'

When it was twenty metres away from me,

a woman suddenly appeared from a large bush, brandishing a pair of scissors. My mind went into overdrive here. She was there to extract painful punishment while Rover feasted on my half-dead carcass. She shouted out and the dog immediately stopped and reluctantly, still eyeing me up, retreated back towards her.

'Sorry about that,' she laughed, not really sorry in the slightest. 'She's very protective of her calves.'

Seeing my bewilderment, she continued, 'Over there,' she pointed, towards a very young calf and its mother standing in the centre of a field. 'It's less than an hour old. Sometimes the dog is wary of anyone getting too close.' The dog, was looking at me with barely concealed hatred and no small amount of smug justification.

'Oh right,' I said, my voice surprisingly high and then stupidly repeating it. 'Oh right. What are you doing?' I asked, trying to sound polite, but instead coming out all accusatory.

'Nothing,' she said guiltily, hiding the scissors behind her back. I continued through the fields.

There were good views now down into Cumbria and as the weather was clear, I could see from the Pennines in the east, over and beyond the buildings of Carlisle towards the Lake District mountains and further west towards the coast. Cumbria is a beautiful county, steeped in history. There has been much debate recently about a potential local government reorganisation, centering on the view that the county is both artificial and too big. Well it is certainly big in terms of size, going from the Scottish border down almost to Lancaster and from the coast in the west to the Pennines in the east. Carlisle, its 'capital' sits in the north-east corner of the county. its second biggest town is Barrow-in-Furness, some eighty five miles away. Although nominally within the north west region, the inhabitants of Carlisle generally have more affinity within those living at the other side of the Wall, rather than Merseyside for example. Manchester is twice as far away as Newcastle from Carlisle.

As regards the accusation of artificial, well which local government boundary isn't? The Wall was the first frontier in this area and its position was defined largely because of geological and geographical rather than ethnological reasons. Modern Cumbria was defined in 1974 by the Local Government Act, but the name dates back at least 1,500 years before that – a fact largely ignored by those currently promoting the 'ancient county of Cumberland' (which, along with Westmorland in the south and east, and bits of Lancashire and Yorkshire, form modern Cumbria).

The word Cumbria is basically the same as that used by the Welsh for their country. It derives from the Cymry, or 'compatriots', a group of Celtic tribes which lived in the area and to the north in southern Scotland. There are similarities in the place-names of both Cumbria and Wales e.g. the Welsh words pen (head or hill) – Penrith, Penruddock; caer (fortress) – Carlisle, Caermote; glyn (valley) – Glencoyne; blaen (top) – Blennerhasset, Blencathra.

Sometime around the late sixth century, the kingdom of Rheged existed in this area, led by Urien (a figure closely associated with some of the stories attributed to King Arthur). Urien succeeded in uniting the British against the Anglo-Saxons who were now based in the east, but rivalry within the native tribes ended in his death. After a battle near Catterick in 600AD, Rheged ceased to be a power, although there is evidence that its descendants held some sort of influence at the Anglo-Saxon Northumbrian court. The battle of Chester in 615 sealed the fate of

British power by driving a wedge between the northern Celts and the Welsh. However although Northumbria effectively controlled what is now northern England, Celtic influences in Cumbria remained for some time and it is not un-useful (although perhaps a bit too romantic) to view Cumbria as a place where a number of 'British' customs, and of course place-names, continued to survive. In 685, King Ecgfrith of Northumbria created the Diocese of Lindisfarne for (later Saint) Cuthbert, which swept along the Scottish borders and down into the Lake District, perhaps an attempt to 'colonise' or at least introduce the British there to English customs. It is interesting to note that modern Cumbria is therefore mainly a mix of Celtic/ British Cymry and the Anglo-Saxon/English Westmaringaland ('the land west of the moors').

The last bit of Wall had been seen at Hare Hill, but just before Walton, at Dovecote Bridge, there is a short, grass-covered stretch. Until recently this was the only bit of red sandstone Wall which was still visible in Cumbria, having been exposed in the mid 1960s. Hunter Davies saw it covered in black tarpaulin when he visited in winter. By 1983 the erosion caused by the weather had so accelerated that it was decided to re-cover it with soil and grass.

Coming into Walton, I made for the Centurion Inn where I had booked a room. The inn lies on top of the Wall and I had heard so many good reports of its food and gossip about how it was near to closing before the trail opened earlier in the year, no doubt an exaggeration (though hopefully not where the food was concerned). Inside, the bar was packed with walkers, including someone whose brother is apparently one of my neighbours, and of course Keith, Connor and Danny. The latter two were out in the garden playing with the house Alsatian, which I was glad to note was inquisitive but friendly.

Keith and his two boys still had another couple of miles to go that day, towards Irthington. It was only three o'clock in the afternoon and he asked me what I was going to do with the rest of my day and I said I would probably have a little walk. At this he started laughing, then I began too and one by one everyone in the pub joined in: a mad cackle of mad hikers, all slightly pissed from their mid-afternoon beer. A middle-aged couple sitting in the corner, slowly getting sloshed and on their third bottle of wine, and the barmaid (texting and receiving so furtively that it must have been illicit) were the only ones who kept a straight, if bemused, face. Even the dog began howling.

After Keith and the boys had left I went up to my room and had a shower, lay on the bed and fell asleep. I was woken up by a call from a friend, Andy, who was coming out to Walton from Carlisle to have a beer with me. That beer turned into another, then some wine and finally a wonderful meal, cooked on the premises. For the rest of the evening, the pub remained pretty quiet, much quieter than the Station Hotel in Gilsland the previous night. We were joined only by the young Dutch couple from Birdoswald, who had been there almost as long as I, plus the (by now) very pissed middle-aged couple, and a couple of other walkers.

Looking around the Centurion, I wondered whether this was the same place where William Hutton had been unable to get any drink other than milk, although it was then a pub known as The Cow and Boot. The family who were tenants or owners there occupied all the rooms. There were, as well as Mum and Dad, six children. One of them, as Hutton says, 'I was sorry to see, was approaching the grave'. I am convinced that it is certainly the place Harrison visited in the 1950s, although it was then known as the Black Bull. His visit was much more pleasant and, like us, he had a lovely meal.

Breakfast was not quite as good as the evening meal. The Dutch couple were similarly disappointed, having also eaten there the night before. Oh well, you can't have everything. The Alsatian nearly did though, as he paced menacingly around us, his nose leading him to the meaty scraps which were being discarded in his direction. It was expensive too, though not as much as New-brough Park; overall, however, I would still recommend at least the evening meal.

8

Walton to Monkhill

Having had an easy time of it the day before, I would now have to walk some seventeen miles, and get to Carlisle by lunchtime, where I had promised to meet some friends from work. I was also sunburnt, a result of the unexpected weather the previous day – although the weather had given up again and there was a steady drizzle as I set off ever westwards, in the general direction of Irthington and Newtown.

I had read something in the official guide book which had worried me throughout the previous evening and had spoiled breakfast. After passing through a wood, the book explains: 'turn right onto the farm road, and at the minor road turn immediately left up the farm track, where a welcoming committee of dogs can usually be found waiting. A dozen or so enormous, salivating, bloodthirsty beasts standing as tall as elephants – you are advised to take a taxi past this point.'

It was only afterwards that I discovered that the last sentence wasn't actually there and must have been the product of my canine paranoia. Having built up the fearsome premonition in such horrendous detail, I was actually overjoyed and grateful to find that only one vicious canine was hurtling along the path towards me, teeth bared, tail down. I waited for his owner (thankfully standing nearby) to call him off and this seemed to take an eternity. Finally, the whistle came, and the dog rushed back towards the farmer, who came over to say hello.

'Hello,' I said. He just looked me up and down, perhaps eyeing up my expensive boots which he would nick should he decide to let his dog murder me.

'Em,' I continued, 'which way do I go now?' This was clearly a stupid question with an obvious answer – the path led either straight through his front door and his house, or continued in the opposite direction towards some fields and a 'Hadrian's Wall Path' signpost. Understandably he looked at me as if I were an imbecile, but decided to play along. He wasn't going to tell me unless I put something in a money box, which was sitting on the fence. I slipped in a £1 coin, and after that he became much friendlier. The money was for the church and he was reluctant to put a sign there asking for a donation, he explained. He pointed me in the (obvious) right direction, advising me that I would soon come to a lovely foot-bridge, crossing the Cam Beck.

Going this way, the path diverts you away from and around the next fort, Camboglanna which probably means something like 'the bank on the river bend' and it has given its name to the beck. The modern name is Castlesteads, also given to the eighteenth century country house which completely destroyed any remains of the fort, a process which had started somewhat earlier with river erosion. There is therefore nothing to see of this fort which is interestingly not on the Wall, but four hundred metres to the south, on a spot where a commanding view would have been possible.

I found the footbridge, as promised, and walked through another farm, thankfully dog-less and with one happy farmer eager to show me the way, shouting out through the window of his 1970s car as he appeared to be practising three-point turns over and over again. In time I came towards the village of Newtown, where the trail takes you right through the end of someone's garden. I wonder what those who live on the Wall actually think of the trail? Throughout I had found nothing but politeness, though I guess there is a realisation that the Wall has brought some business to the area, particularly welcome after the experience of foot and mouth, two years previously. I had had my suspicions of farmers in the early stages where fresh and strong nettles and holly enveloped the ground around some of the foot path and stiles, but so far none had come at me with a shotgun. All had called their dogs off when they noticed my imminent mauling. I hadn't even seen any bulls, carelessly left on the trail, although there had been that sign back at

Banks, near the Signal Station.

In Newtown, I crossed the Longtown-Brampton road (being only two miles from the latter) and passed down a street of affluent houses and exited the village through a field. I was still on the course of the Wall and could clearly make out the ditch just to my right. Light aircraft were now buzzing around me, as to my left was Carlisle Airport. When I first came to Carlisle, it was possible to do day return trips to Reykjavick from here, but then it all went quiet. A few years ago, the airport was bought by Edward Haughey, an Irish politician and businessman, who also owns Corby Castle, a few miles further west, and who has started to expand the small airport. Regular flights to London have been mentioned, though I still quite fancy the day trip to Iceland idea myself. Someone once told me that Carlisle Airport's runway was built long enough to enable such huge creatures as Concorde to land there if necessary. As I wrote this book a couple of months after finishing my walk, Concorde made its last ever flight.

Having passed the runways and the hamlet of Old Wall, and with nothing more taxing to do than keep walking in a straight line, I suddenly became aware that I was lost. I remember the guide book telling me to turn right and cross a field, or something like that, although afterwards I noticed that these words have somehow disappeared from my edition. As I criss-crossed the field, like a wild animal looking for a way out, I heard voices back up near the ditch and assumed it would be the Dutch couple. I planned to let them take the lead and follow their Friesian efficiency.

There were in fact three figures ahead however, not two: it was clearly Keith, Connor and Danny again, so I caught up with them much to Keith's surprise, 'You must have been moving quickly. When I looked back a minute ago, there was no-one behind us.' I didn't tell him I had been pacing around the perimeter of the adjoining field.

We continued walking together, meeting two or three dogs, which the kids fortunately took care off, and a dead rat the size of a Daschund. Just after Wall Head, the three others continued on the trail down to Crosby, but I wanted to stay faithful to the line and walked towards Walby. From here I passed by Wallfoot (are you getting the pattern of place names here?) and again, ignoring the trail, which goes off down through Linstock and Rickerby Park, followed the old Brampton Road, across the roundabout (which is signposted to Scotland), into Carlisle. On the right hand side is Hadrian's Camp, once fittingly an army camp, but now a place for Travellers.

To my left were some seriously lovely houses – this is one of the nicest and most expensive areas of the city – and beyond them the River Eden, meandering through Rickerby Park. I was hurrying now, as it was way past twelve o'clock, but took some time to glance over to my right, as I passed the art college – the sight of the largest and most important fort of the Wall at Stanwix. Originally known as Uxellodonum ('High Fort')' and then Petriana, it was 9.3 acres in size (i.e. 590m by 590m) and held the only one thousand strong cavalry garrison in Britain, which guarded the Eden bridgehead.

I followed the modern bridge across the river and entered the city. Carlisle is a very old place. Already a native settlement before the Romans came, the Roman general Agricola also established a base there, when he arrived some time after 78AD. This base was known as Luguvalium, a name which, despite its second part, has nothing to do with Wall. It means something like 'the stronghold of Lugus', who was a Celtic god, often identified with the Roman god Mercury. When the Romans moved on into Scotland, a garrison was left behind in a wooden fort which was built roughly between where the cathedral and castle are now. The Romans soon gave up on Scotland and strengthened the fort at Carlisle sometime after 100AD. The Stanegate was constructed, stretching east from here, through Crosby, Vindolanda and Newburgh, all the way to Corbridge. When the Wall was built, the fort at Luguvalium was demolished and the army moved to Stanwix. Instead Carlisle became a civil and administrative centre, with well-built houses, a public water system (still in operation and seen some six hundred years later by St. Cuthbert), markets, cemeteries and of course all under the protection of the biggest army in Britain, stationed nearby.

When the Romans left, Carlisle appears to have remained an important civilian and perhaps Christian centre – hence Cuthbert's visits – and at some point the name Luguvalium turned first into Luel and then the prefix 'Caer-', Celtic for 'fortress' was added. Carlisle then became at different points part of Northumbria, then Strathclyde, then part of a Cumbrian kingdom. All this is very hazy, and this is not the place for a detailed study.

We do know however that by the time of the Norman Conquest (1066), Carlisle was part of Scotland, as was much of present-day Cumbria – this area does not appear in the Domesday Book, which of course related only to England. In 1092, King William Rufus took the town and built a strong Norman keep there on the site of the present-day castle. Carlisle thus became the last English city, although it has passed between the two countries a few times since then. Its proximity to Scotland has not diminished its sense of identity – perhaps even strengthened it – but there is an inevitable mix of accents around the place. One of the most surprising phenomena about the border here is in fact the sudden change of accent which occurs a few miles to the north, where Scotland begins. The southern Scottish accent is one of the strongest and although quite distinct from the Glasgow-Edinburgh-central-belt accents, is obviously identifiable as Scots. This change begins immediately at Gretna – there is no gradual lengthening of vowels, no slow hardening of consonants – it's quite simply over the bridge and wham, straight into another country with its pound notes, different kinds of flyers and tenners, more sensible house-buying system and sharp

Scottish pronunciations. There is more distinction and variation of accent in the mile between Metal Bridge (just south of the Border) and Gretna than there is in the hundred miles to the south.

I hurried past the city council-owned Sands Centre and into the city, meeting the lunch-time crowds – of which I am usually part. You often see the same people day in, day out, doing the same things, going to the same baker's shops and ordering the same sandwich, then buying the same newspaper. The females usually never wear the same outfit on consecutive days; the men in suits usually change their tie. Everyone has the same air of indifference. There is a silent acknowledge-ment of everyone else's presence, not acted upon, until one of us gets confused and, having seen that person in the same place at the same time, mixes him/her up with someone they actually know and attempts to initiate a conversation. The embarrassment and sense of harassment on the other face quickly dispels any such foolish thoughts and the exchange is aborted, though all done in a stranger's cloud of politeness.

When I first came to Carlisle, I was taken aback by the legendary friendliness of 'them up north'. For example, one thing it took me some time to get used to was that everyone thanked the bus driver when leaving the bus. People do say hello when you pass them out in the villages – actually here they usually ask. 'How are you doing?' No answer is expected, other than perhaps a repetition of the original question, something which is open to misinterpretation on the part of an 'outsider'. Having lived here for some time now I have got into the way of asking people I know 'how they are doing.' On one occasion, with a non-Cumbrian who had been here for only three months or so, this resulted in a long and unlooked-for ramble about the difficulties of selling his house down south, finding a gym in Carlisle and the olfactory problems of his boss. Nowadays, unless I know they are locally-bred, I restrict myself to 'hello.'

Reaching the centre of Carlisle, and walking through the Lanes Shopping Centre, I became aware that the silent acknowledgement game was being played slightly differently. People clearly recognised me, but they seemed to be having a problem transferring the usual pale-faced, suited office worker into this suntanned, unshaven (for seven days) hobo, wearing shorts and expensive, muddy walking boots and carrying a rucksack half his size. Some of them caught my eye with disbelief, others with revulsion. Some, mainly guys, definitely showed a little jealousy, others, mainly women, with admiration and barely-concealed desire. Or so I pretended. I walked towards Leonardo's. the wine bar/pub/restaurant opposite the bus station and met up with Tony, Dave and Jen. Having walked around eleven miles that morning, I more than deserved a refreshing pint of good German beer – Warsteiner – and a spicy chicken sandwich.

Leaving the pub (after a sickly Irish coffee, which someone thought would help me on my way). I bumped into a couple of other friends, both of whom seemed astonished at what I was doing. No, not the idea of the walk, just that I was now walking the five or so miles to Monkhill to spend the night at Tony's house. This was, they thought, a dangerous idea, given that I still had the last part of the trail to do, the next morning.

But I still had some more walking that day and the anaesthetic effect of Warsteiner would soon wear off. The sun had also come out, in other circumstances a good thing, but the Irish coffee was in danger of reacting badly to the heat. Nevertheless, I struggled on.

The Wall crossed the River Eden here with a bridge. On the southern bank a number of stones, thought to be Roman, have been piled up where it is thought the bridge may have been. This was definitely the last possible piece of Wall I would see, though slightly artificial in its set-up. Sadly, the sign, which I presume would have explained the background to the bridge abutment, had been vandalised and this rather depressed me. I was already feeling a bit mournful: tonight would be my last night, tomorrow the last day, no more Wall to see, Irish coffee not settling down, and now this small piece of destruction, something I had not encountered anywhere else. Walking through the less affluent areas of Newcastle and Newburn or the remote and windy landscapes of Sewingshields, all previous markers and signposts had been left in place. Here, in the award-winning Bitts Park, right in the middle of pretty little Carlisle, next to the empty cans and used condoms, were the unreadable fragments of the notice. Perhaps I was over reacting, but I felt a little bit of the anger that Harrison had spent his week on the Wall exorcising, and began to look for deeper theories to all of this. Carlisle is, as I say, a pretty little city, in an enviable location. Close to the Lakes, the sea, the Eden Valley, the Borders, the Wall; the Eden runs through the middle, lush parks on both sides; an almost European-style vast pedestrian centre, with cafes and mock medieval buildings. Underneath though perhaps still lies some of the Reiver mentality, the war and strife that has lasted two thousand years, which manifests itself in such things as the constant and relentless destruction of the bus stop in my village, the violence to city centre property and humans after eleven o'clock on a Friday night, and of course this small piece of vandalism near the pile of Roman stones.

Harrison had taken me over. I moved swiftly on.

Those last few paragraphs of moralistic diatribe were written, as much of this book has been, in the early hours of each morning, before having breakfast and going off to work. It's difficult trying to be a writer and keep a full time job going, and it had taken me nearly two months of writing what I had walked in five days. My thoughts on the underlying border violence within the Carlisle character were written on the morning of 21 October 2003.

On that Tuesday morning, a few hours

later, a neighbour on the less than pleasant Raffles estate, in the west of the city, watched a young mother and her ten month old baby leave their house. She stopped and spoke to the couple, trying unsuccessfully to get the baby to smile at her. An hour or so later, the mother and baby were in Gregg's Bakery, at the bottom of Scotch Street in the city centre, when the baby's father turned up and thrust a knife through the throat and neck of the ten-month-old, killing the boy outright and injuring his mother, before running off towards the centre, where he was soon caught.

The murder made the national news as well as local. On this painful day, Carlisle was described bizarrely as an 'unremarkable town', and on the BBC Website, the story referred to, 'the former Roman stronghold of Carlisle,' a coincidental but poignant reference to the words I had written only a few hours earlier.

As the people of Carlisle picked up the late editions with the photo of the boy smiling out (the photo had been entered in the paper's Bonny Baby competition only two months earlier), we all tried to come to terms with what had happened in our 'unremarkable town'. When it became clear shortly after-

wards that the father, accused of the stabbing, was an illegal immigrant, facing deport-
ation to Bangladesh that same week, there
was somehow amid the sadness a tiny, but
important, sense of relief that he was an outsider, not one of them. Within a few more
days, the topic of discussion had moved on
further still to whether the bakery should
have re-opened so quickly, the hundreds of
bouquets and cuddly toys having been
removed.

As it happens, I had actually walked past the
bakery two months earlier, on my way into
Carlisle, unaware as we all were of the
horrors which would later to unfold. I also
walked past it a second time on way back to
the trail and Bitts Park, where I had seen the
vandalised sign near the abutment. I walked
through the outer reaches of the park,
alongside the river, presented with the usual
mixture of foul-smelling wild plants and
discarded lager cans often found in places
you never knew existed. There was the
obligatory solitary glove or car foot mat too,
giving the place an air of abandon and
disuse. The air was further sullied by the
nearby sewage works and dump.

A number of railway bridges crossed the

river here – Carlisle was once a very important railway centre, with stations belonging to many of the different railway companies which used it. This was of course in the days before nationalisation, subsequent privatisation and subsequent partial-nationalisation again. As with the outskirts of Newcastle, Carlisle's suburbs were populated by the huge pylons. They reminded me of an enemy force, standing erect and awaiting orders to invade the city. Unlike their eastern cousins however, these pylons were silent: there was no buzzing, an effect which just added to their menace.

I passed alongside a small hamlet which according to the map is called 'Knockupworth Cottage'. Now, every place on earth has its silly names (the best clearly being 'Truth or Consequences' in New Mexico, allegedly named after a TV quiz show), but Cumbria does seem to have a disproportionately large number of them.

As well as Knockupworth, there is a Great Cockup and a Little Cockup (both near Bassenthwaite), Cumcatch, west of Brampton, Haggbeck (near Longtown), Ponsonby, down in the west and the ungrateful village of Unthank, south of Carlisle. The unfathomable Curly Job Well is near to Caldbeck, whilst down in the Lakes proper you can find a mountain called 'High Street' and also the following places:

Hobgrumble Gill, Apronful of Stones, Red Covercloth, Fisher's Wife's Rake, Cuddyarch Sough, Burnt Horse and Captain Whelter's Bog. Nearer to the Wall there's a Talkin Head. Yes, Northumbria with its Once and Twice Brewed has nothing on the Cumbrians.

Suitably and childishly amused, I passed on towards the village of Grinsdale and out through it towards Kirkandrews-on-Eden. Walking though a field I saw a large cow blocking the footstile at the opposite end. As I approached, the cow made no attempt to move, although it did start staring at me with the usual reticent curiosity which I had come to know from such beasts. I thought to myself how much experience I now had of sheep and cattle, and how I had actually been wary of them at first. Now I felt fairly convinced that I knew how to deal with these harmless docile beasts. The only thing to be wary of was when there were any calves nearby – the animals can be unpredictable then. As I looked round I was at first relieved to see that there were no calves in the field, and then bemused to notice that there were in fact no other animals at all in the field. With dawning horror, I looked at the underside of the 'cow' – no udder, but something else. I froze, properly scared now. I considered backing off, but really there was no alternative other than a very long detour. Noting that the animal had no horns, I calculated that if I edged around it very gently, I might be able to get to the stile, without upsetting it. Besides, if it did suddenly move, I reckoned I would have enough fear and adrenalin to vault over the one and a half metre high fence. As it was, the animal watched me intently as I passed slowly by, but made no sudden moves.

I crossed over, relieved that I had survived and looking forward to embellishing my bravado at a future date, when I came to the next field, with a sign next to the stile: 'Danger: Bull in Field'. Shit. The fear returned. This was really bad luck. I stood up on the stile and saw that there was nothing in the field, but also was aware that the field rose up to a peak halfway along and then dropped down towards some farm buildings. Perhaps the bull was down there?

I had no choice however but to walk quickly (on tiptoe actually) alongside the boundary (I would have had no problem in jumping over the fence there, but neither, presumably, would a determined bull) towards the next field. As I neared my target and crossed over the brow of the hill, there standing at the bottom was a massive white bull, gazing at me and, I swear, snorting fire. This time there were horns. I froze. The bull started walking towards me. I ran at top speed. I have no idea if he quickened his pace and began chasing me because I ran the next fifty metres in about three seconds and carried on running though the next field and then through the next until I reached a little lane at the edge of the village of Kirkandrews. In my haste I had forgotten to look for evidence of the Vallum which is apparent here and also to stop and chuckle at the place named 'Sourmilk Bridge'.

Having had enough of farms, I decided not to follow the trail which takes you back down through arable land to the river and Beaumont, but instead to walk towards the main road and thence the final half mile to Monkhill. As I would be walking on the Vallum, I felt no further justifications was needed.

During that final half mile I was made aware of where the 'hill' in Monkhill comes from. The sun had finally taken over the sky and I was hot, thirsty and with aching feet once again, having walked my furthest daily journey. I stopped at the Drover's Rest for a glass of water and desperate toilet stop, before walking round to Tony's house. In the pub, after checking any potentially embarrassing bull-initiated accidents (none, thankfully, but you can never be too sure, especially when your whole body has gone numb), I was engaged in conversation by a young girl (aged about six) who showed me her Barbie watch and asked if I had one. When I told her I didn't wear a watch, she asked me what time I was going home. 'Tomorrow,' I said, sad that my journey was almost over. As I left (her parents need not have looked so openly relieved), the little girl came over to me, 'You can't sleep here you know.'

Well, not exactly, but Tony and I did return there later that night, accompanied by Keith (another one – not the walker), who had driven out from Carlisle. It's no surprise how soundly you can sleep after a few beers and seventeen miles of walking.

9

Monkhill to Bowness

The last day dawned fine and dry and as Tony went off to his work in Carlisle, I stepped out into the sun for the final six miles of the adventure. A mile or so after walking dangerously on the main road, the line of the Wall comes back down towards the Vallum at the village of Burgh-by-Sands, pronounced as at Newbrough, as 'Bruff'. There was also a Roman fort here, this time on the Wall, and known as Aballava, or 'apple orchard'. There is very little evidence left to suggest that this affluent village was once a Roman military camp, although there are clues in the building work of St Michael's Church, which contains some of the Roman stones. This church is made up partly of a pele tower, evidence again of border strife, but not originally the Reivers this time.

The trouble dates back to the end of the thirteenth century. Edward I, the so-called 'Hammer of the Scots', was actually relatively unsuccessful with his invasions over the border. Despite heavy taxes on his English subjects, he led the country deeply into debt, and by the time of his death in 1307, he had added Wales to his reign but not Scotland. For the next two hundred years, subsequent English kings attempted to carry on what Edward had started, but never quite succeeded, although the south of Scotland and north of England became a very dangerous place to live. At first the danger was a symptom of the wars between the two countries; later it was a result of the Reivers who, as we have seen, had little care for the nationalist cause on either side. Ironically, the dispute finally ended when the Scottish King, James VI, was invited to be King James I of England, thus uniting the two kingdoms.

Edward I actually died here (of dysentery) at Burgh-by-Sands, whilst waiting to cross the Solway and invade Scotland once again. A monument nearby marks the spot. Being Scottish, I declined to pay my respects.

Further on, past Longburgh, a cattle grid signalled the entrance to the salty Solway Marshes. To my right was the firth itself, at (very) low tide, showing how it would have been perfectly possible to walk across to

Scotland – providing of course that you knew how to navigate the incoming tides, which can be horrifically fast. At high tide, this seems like a sensible place to have ended the Wall. The shore on the other side is a good couple of miles away. But the Romans had obviously seen what I did that morning; the tide was out and the bay looked like no more than a large beach. To my left was a high mound, accompanying the road as far as I could see, towards Port Carlisle, and at first I automatically assumed that this had something to do with the Wall. However, I had long since finished seeing evidence of the barrier (at least 'in situ') some time ago, and this was in fact the remains of the railway line. Before that it had been something much more exciting – but more of that later.

The marshes were covered with grazing sheep and cattle – once again emphasising the importance of farming in this region. I thought of how deserted this scene would have been a couple of years ago during the foot and mouth epidemic, and gave an involuntary shudder.

Further east, farmers are being encouraged to help preserve the Wall and Vallum through Defra's Countryside Stewardship Scheme which has been drawn up with the support of

English Heritage's Hadrian's Wall Co-ordination Unit. Some features of the Vallum have been shown to be at risk from ploughing and the intensification of agriculture since 1945, which has caused more damage in the past six decades than in the previous six centuries. The unit is eager not to apportion blame to the farmers – we must all share that with our demand for more and cheaper food.

Another similar scheme is the Drovers Project, launched in February 2003 by a partnership between English Heritage, the Heritage Lottery Fund, English Nature, the Countryside Agency and the National Trust. This project encourages farmers to reintroduce traditional types of cattle to the region, cattle which are recognised for their ability to graze rough grasslands and control invasive species of grass (such as purple moor grass, also known as white or bent grass) and bracken. These grasses are very competitive – the plant equivalent of the grey squirrel – and tend to dominate the less competitive plants. The first Drovers Project site was established at Hotbank Farm on the Wall, midway between Housesteads and Once Brewed.

I passed through the village of Drumburgh, which was once the site of the smallest fort on the Wall. Until this year, its Roman name was believed to be Congavata, the meaning of which has become lost through the centuries. Following the finding of the bowl in Staffordshire, it is possible that it may have been known as Coggabata. Originally this was a turf fort, but later rebuilt in stone. There is one building of note in the village – the so-called Drumburgh Castle, which is in fact a sixteenth century manor house, built almost entirely out of red sandstone from the Wall.

Finally I came to the small village once known as Fisher's Cross. In 1795, an engineer called William Chapman proposed that a canal be built from Newcastle to the Solway Firth at Maryport, via Carlisle. This was an ambitious project which would also be linked to Ullswater, west of Penrith, and would cost only £3,000 (or £170k in today's money) per mile or £195,000 in total (for 65 miles). His business plan estimated that annual income would be £17,242, and the canal would pay for itself sooner or later. Very few took him seriously and those who did said that his estimates only equated to around twenty per cent of the actual costs. The plan therefore went no further.

However in 1817, a group, headed by the MP Sir James Graham, asked Chapman to produce some estimates and a survey for a possible canal from Carlisle to the Solway. Chapman's ambition was stirred again and as well as producing a plan for a canal running from Fisher's Cross into Carlisle, this, he said, would only be the start and soon the canal would extend eastwards and south to Penrith. The Carlisle-Solway canal was enough at this stage however and a special Act of Parliament was passed just two years later to authorise its building. The final cost was £20,000 higher than Chapman's original estimate, finally coming to £90,000 (a very cheap £3.7m if inflated to today's levels). The eleven mile long building work took four years and on 12 March 1823, the Carlisle Canal Committee finished their pub breakfast and travelled (by road) to Fisher's Cross, which had now been renamed Port Carlisle. At ten o'clock in the morning, the committee stepped on board the *Robert Burns*, the first ship in the inaugural flotilla, and set sail for the city.

The banks of the canal were lined with crowds, who were getting steadily inebriated. One spectator, 'who had been far too liberal with refreshments,' as the local paper, the *Carlisle Patriot*, put it, fell into the canal. He survived, ending up only with, 'a taste of early spring bathing against his will.' Another old man, 97 years old, ill and utterly bedridden, was pushed down to the canal, still in his bed. The flotilla reached Carlisle just before three o'clock, to the strains of *Rule Britannia* and *God Save The King*, whereupon the committee marched back to the pub they had started in (The Bush) and drank on and into the next morning at the place which later became the Crown and Mitre.

At first the canal was extremely successful; the price of freight dropped (in the case of coal by nearly fifty per cent) and a passenger service from Carlisle through the canal to Liverpool was very well-used, taking little more than ten hours. By 1839, over one thousand German immigrants passed through the canal in one month (June), on their way to a new life in the United States. This was the best year for the canal, and things went downhill from here. In 1845 the Maryport and Carlisle Railway was completed, taking freight more quickly to the Cumbrian coast. In 1847, the Lancaster and Carlisle Railway initiated a service from Carlisle to Liverpool and in 1848, the Carlisle and Annan Navigation Company threw in the towel, itself becoming a railway company. In 1854 the canal was drained and a railway track laid down. Legend has it that during this draining a massive eel was found which was later eaten at the city's corporation dinner, in remembrance of Chapman's dream.

The new venture forgot any loyalty to the village the canal had created. Another railway company, the North British, extended the line down to Silloth, which thus became the new 'port' for Carlisle and in 1869, the Caledonian Railway Company built a viaduct from Bowness to Annan in Scotland, thus bypassing the old Fisher's Cross completely. This viaduct only lasted until 1914 (being demolished twenty one years later). The railway line from Port Carlisle to its mother city was finally closed in 1932.

In 1996, the idea of creating a much larger version of the canal – from the Solway to the Tyne – was put forward once again. I remember it hit the headlines of the local and national press, and, buying a house at the time on what was near to the proposed route, my lawyer in Cambridge urged me to hesitate before committing myself. The canal would use the River Tyne as far as possible and then cut across the country to the south of Hadrian's Wall. It would be used, like the Caledonian canal in Scotland, for movement of freight between Europe and the Atlantic, without the need to use the busy route around the south of England, or the often dangerous one around the north of Scotland. A figure of £6 billion was mentioned. Nothing came of it.

Annoyingly I paid too much attention to the official trail at this point of my walk and so completely bypassed Port Carlisle. The trail takes you down an overgrown path, behind the gardens of the village houses, and you only emerge once the village is behind you. It is a shame to miss out on the Victorian houses, the remains of the station platform and a small Roman altar built into the doorway of one of the houses – though I understand that they are trying to take you away from the road. I was a bit pissed off to say the least, so walked back and through the village, making my point, willing someone to ask me why I had departed from the proper trail. Then I realised I had only one mile left to walk.

One final mile. I wanted it to be long. I wanted it to be spectacular and in a certain way it was, though it had nothing to do with anything the Romans had control over. As I looked over the Solway into Scotland, I noticed that the tide was starting to come in. It was the noise at first, which began as a gentle swish of the tide and then got louder, a higher pitch, and then dropped down again as the estuary filled up at an astonishing rate. You may have heard, like I had, the warnings of the tide coming in more quickly than a galloping horse. Until I saw what was happening to my right that day I would have dismissed this as hyperbole, but it was actually quite breathtaking. If you'd been out there, halfway across what had appeared to be a beach and this happened, you'd be swept aside. The gulls and other birds I cannot name were going mad, almost drowning out the noise of the waves. By the time I reached Bowness, the beach was no more; it was a deep, dark, threatening and deathly calm again, sea.

Another association of Bowness with mortality is referred to by Jessie Mothersole who met a (in her case only one) fat lady on a train, having finished her walk. On hearing that Jessie had been to Burgh-by-Sands, the fatty said, 'Ah I know it well; I've been to many a funeral there. They bury them there from Glasson, and from Drumburgh, and I think from Kirkbride. It's a nice place, Bowness, to be buried.'

Oh yes?

'I'd as lief be buried there myself,' continued the lady. 'My husband's father, he was a canal man, lived for twenty years on a houseboat on the canal and he's buried at Bowness.'

It was the end of the Wall, and originally sited the second largest fort (after Stanwix), known then as Maia (probably meaning 'the bigger/larger'). This fort overlooked the sea and would have provided excellent views across the Solway. Sadly nothing now survives. From here down the Solway coast the Romans built a series of fortlets and milecastles which kept an eye on an attack coming up the Solway or over from Scotland. However, my Wall walk ended here and I did something I hadn't done since Wallsend – I got the second stamp on my 'passport'. I made my way to the Kings Arms for a well-deserved beer and there eating plates of chips were Keith, Connor and Danny. They were waiting for the Hadrian's Wall bus, the 'AD 122', which would take them back to where they had left their car in Wallsend. It would be an interesting, but long, ride, passing through the places they had walked over the past seven or eight days. I said my goodbyes and hopped on the local bus into Carlisle, with the sea, and Scotland and the edge of the Roman Empire, marked out by the Great Wall of Britain, all to my left now.

POSTSCRIPT

The Romanway Guest House, Gilsland, reference page 157: On 30 July 2004, the *Cumberland News* reported that Carlisle City Council had ordered the owner of the Romanway to make a number of improvements and clean up the premises.

Murder in Carlisle bakery, reference page 203: On Wednesday 28 July 2004, a forty year old illegal immigrant was jailed for life for the murder of his baby son in Carlisle in 2003. The Judge handed down a minimum sentence of twelve years. In September 2004, it was announced that the Court of Appeal would look into the sentencing, after concerns about it being too lenient.

Birdoswald Fort, reference page 175: In September 2004, Cumbria County Council decided to hand over Birdoswald Roman Fort to English Heritage. There was a nominal fee in recognition of the investment put in by the county council over the last twenty years

The publishers hope that this book has given you enjoyable reading. Large Print Books are especially designed to be as easy to see and hold as possible. If you wish a complete list of our books please ask at your local library or write directly to:

Dales Large Print Books
Magna House, Long Preston,
Skipton, North Yorkshire.
BD23 4ND

This Large Print Book, for people
who cannot read normal print,
is published under the auspices of

THE ULVERSCROFT FOUNDATION

... we hope you have enjoyed this book.
Please think for a moment about those
who have worse eyesight than you ...
and are unable to even read or enjoy
Large Print without great difficulty.

You can help them by sending a
donation, large or small, to:

**The Ulverscroft Foundation,
1, The Green, Bradgate Road,
Anstey, Leicestershire, LE7 7FU,
England.**
or request a copy of our brochure for
more details.

The Foundation will use all donations
to assist those people who are visually
impaired and need special attention
with medical research, diagnosis
and treatment.

Thank you very much for your help.